Dennis Sweetland

MARK

From Death to Life

New City Press

Published in the United States by New City Press
202 Cardinal Rd., Hyde Park, NY 12538
©2000 Dennis Sweetland

Cover design by Nick Cianfarani

Library of Congress Cataloging-in-Publication Data:
Sweetland, Dennis M.
    Mark : from death to life / Dennis Sweetland.
        p. cm. -- (Spiritual commentaries)
    Includes bibliographical references.
    ISBN 1-56548-117-8
    1. Bible. N.T. Mark--Commentaries. I. Title II. Series.

BS2585.3. S94 2000
226.3'07--dc21   99-086160

Printed in Canada

Contents

Introduction

According to tradition, the earliest Christian message began to take shape in Jerusalem immediately after the crucifixion of Jesus (ca. 33 C.E.). When he was executed, Jesus' followers fled or hid, but their hopes were renewed when they saw him alive again. They were convinced that the kingdom he had spoken about would appear soon, and that Jesus himself would return too. Having settled down in Jerusalem to wait, these disciples, many of whom had traveled with Jesus throughout his public ministry, told anyone who would listen about what Jesus had said and done. They were eager to convince others that Jesus was the Messiah of Israel and that he would return soon to establish the kingdom of God.

When these initial followers first presented Jesus' message to the world, they used the spoken word. The first Christian kerygma (proclamation about Jesus) was thus entirely oral. It is unlikely that any of Jesus' original followers thought about writing a story of his life. They expected his return in the immediate future, and the question of how best to preserve these stories of and about Jesus did not arise. Thus, Jesus' first disciples preached about him and about his message, and they did so in a Galilean dialect of Aramaic, the same language that Jesus himself had spoken.

Many responded to this early Christian preaching about the good news of salvation with faith. They came to believe that Jesus was the promised Messiah, the Son of God, and that salvation was possible for those who repented and believed. These new believers were then baptized, and thus they joined Jesus' original followers as members of this new community gathered in his name. Some of these converts, who had not known Jesus during his lifetime, began in turn to relate to those they would meet the stories about Jesus. Thus, the number of missionaries grew and the area they covered widened. The language of their preaching changed from Aramaic to Greek, the dominant language of the day.

While the primary means of transmitting these stories about Jesus was oral, there is evidence that some of them might have been written down during this period from 33 to 70 C.E. It appears that usually they were groups of stories dealing with similar topics, such as healings or debates with opponents, that were circulated among various Christian communities. There might also have been written collections of parables or sayings, and some believe that the passion narrative existed in written form during this time. It was not until almost forty years after Jesus' death, however, that the first gospel was written.

The Writing of Mark's Gospel

Mark's importance for the history of Christianity can hardly be overrated. Either slightly before or shortly after 70 C.E., Mark put together various oral and possibly written sources in order to speak to his contemporaries about Jesus and his message. In Mark's Gospel, the Jesus

10

tradition, previously handed down primarily in oral form, appears for the first time in the shape of a book, a fixed written form. The result was a story similar to a Greek biography that appears to have been intended for a Hellenistic (Greek speaking) audience.

While historically this was an event of enormous importance, it is unlikely that Mark saw his work as something radically new. Like his predecessors, he was collecting and preserving various stories about Jesus that were circulating in oral or written form. The difference was that he was preserving them in the written form of a book that appears to describe the career of Jesus. The aim of both Mark and the earlier missionaries was to make available to their audiences the saving message of the crucified and risen Lord.

At this point several questions naturally arise: (1) What do we know about the author of this earliest continuous narrative of Jesus' career? Who was Mark? (2) What do we know about the intended audience? To whom was Mark writing? (3) What led Mark to arrange this material about Jesus in the form of an extended written narrative?

According to tradition, Mark was once a traveling companion of Paul and became the secretary and interpreter of Peter. He is usually identified as John Mark, in whose mother's house (at Jerusalem) Christians assembled (Acts 12:12). This Mark was a cousin of Barnabas (Col 4:10) and accompanied Barnabas and Paul on a missionary journey (Acts 12:25; 13:3; 15:36-39). He appears in Pauline letters (Phlm 24; 2 Tm 4:11) and with Peter (1 Pt 5:13). Papias (ca. 135 C.E.), an early Christian writer who was bishop of Hierapolis in Asia Minor, described Mark as Peter's "interpreter," who based his account on Peter's reminiscences of Jesus. According to the early church historian Eusebius of Caesarea, Papias also notes that Mark "had not heard the Lord or been one of his followers" so that his Gospel lacked "a systematic arrangement of the Lord's sayings."

Careful study of Mark's Gospel has convinced most New Testament scholars that it does not derive from a single apostolic source, such as Peter. As noted earlier, there is widespread agreement that Mark created his Gospel from a variety of oral and perhaps some written collections of material about what Jesus had said and done. There is no internal evidence that would indicate the identity of the sacred writer, and our author never identifies himself. Therefore, the book is usually seen as anonymous; we do not know who wrote this Gospel. There is little doubt that someone named Mark was a follower of Paul and possibly Peter, but we cannot be sure that he wrote the Gospel that has come to bear his name.

Our author, who we will continue to refer to as Mark, offers us few hints about where or for whom he wrote. However, what is often helpful in trying to answer these questions is one of the main themes of the Gospel. Virtually all readers will notice Mark's insistence that following Jesus demands a willingness to suffer for one's faith. This suggests that the Gospel was intended for Christians who were undergoing some type of persecution and needed encouragement to remain faithful.

Tradition tells us that Mark wrote his Gospel in Rome after Peter's death. During the mid-sixties of the first century, the emperor Nero's attack on the Christian community at Rome resulted in numerous Roman Christians being crucified or burned to death. Second-century sources indicate that Peter was martyred during Nero's persecution of the Christians (ca. 64-65 C.E.). However, we cannot be absolutely certain that this Gospel was composed in the late sixties at Rome. More recently there has been a growing number of scholars who argue for Syria or Palestine as the site of the community for which Mark wrote. The Jewish Revolt against Rome (66-73 C.E.) would provide the immediate context for the suffering of the Christian community. These followers of Jesus were in a particularly difficult position, because the Romans regarded them as Jews, and the Jews considered the Christians to be unbelievers. Those supporting a Syria-Palestine location for the Markan community usually suggest that the Gospel was written shortly before or shortly after the destruction of Jerusalem by the Roman army in 70 C.E.

In most commentaries today one can thus expect to find the author claiming that Mark was written by an anonymous Christian shortly before or shortly after 70 C.E. either in Rome or in the Syria-Palestine region. Its audience seems to have been Gentile, unfamiliar with Jewish customs (cf. Mk 7:3-4, 11). Between Nero's first official persecution of Christians (64 C.E.) and the Roman destruction of Jerusalem (70 C.E.), the Christian community faced a series of crises that threatened its survival. Responding to wars, revolts, and persecutions that affected his community, Mark composed a narrative account of Jesus' public career that was very relevant to the circumstances his intended readers faced. The book aimed to equip such Christians to stand firm and remain faithful in the face of persecution (13:9-13).

Since the good news about Jesus had been transmitted

13

orally for almost four decades before Mark wrote his Gospel, one needs to ask what would have led Mark to place the Jesus tradition in this written framework. Several possibilities exist: (1) The ever-growing church would have needed someone to relate the Jesus story in a logical fashion. It is likely that the stories about Jesus circulated originally without an interpretive framework. In other words, each story was a self-contained unit. Unless it was central to the story itself, the exact setting of any particular episode in the ministry of Jesus was not part of the oral tradition. Mark's contribution, then, would have been to provide this larger interpretive framework. (2) The death of the eyewitnesses to the historical ministry of Jesus would have suggested that someone write an account of Jesus' words and deeds while some of these eyewitnesses were still alive. (3) As more time separated Christians from the historical ministry of Jesus, there would have been a desire on the part of these later Christians to know more about Jesus. (4) An internal crisis such as the question about the place of Judaism within Christianity could have precipitated the writing of this Gospel. Or (5) an external crisis such as the Jewish war with Rome could have provided the impetus for Mark to write his account of the life of Jesus.

Regardless of his reason for writing, the result is clear. Mark has gathered together these traditional episodes from the life of Jesus and put them in a larger interpretive framework. Mark's story about Jesus, from his baptism to his death and resurrection, provided his audience with an updated story about Jesus that was relevant to their own time and place. He linked the words of Jesus with his deeds and presented the story of Jesus in narrative form.

Mark, the First Gospel

While once Matthew was assumed to be the first Gospel, today New Testament scholarship accepts that Mark's Gospel was not only the first to be written but that it also served as a source for both Matthew and Luke. There are strong arguments for the chronological priority of Mark. Three of the reasons scholars usually cite are:

1. With almost negligible exceptions, all the narrative material in Mark is found in Matthew and/or Luke.

2. Mark's order of events generally is followed by Matthew and Luke. Whenever all three fail to agree, at least one of the other two nearly always agrees with Mark. When there is a deviation, it can usually be explained quite easily.

3. The far-reaching agreement in wording.

The earlier theory, that Mark is a later work consisting of excerpts from Matthew and Luke, is no longer considered credible by the vast majority of scholars. Among other things, it does not satisfactorily explain why Mark would have selected what he did, leaving out so much material from Matthew and Luke.

In spite of Mark's enormous influence on the Christian tradition, the full extent of his creativity has been appreciated only recently. At the beginning of the twentieth century, Mark was regarded as presenting nothing but a straightforward life of Jesus. While it did not contain an infancy narrative nor provide many details which historians would like to know, by and large it did give the main outline of Jesus' career. Mark was thus taken seriously only as a biography of Jesus; it was seen as historical in its intention.

15

With the advent of Form Criticism (the attempt to discover the oldest oral forms lying behind the written texts of the Gospel), scholars came to the conclusion that Mark does not give a "life of Jesus." There is in fact no attempt to present one incident after another in the order in which they happened historically. With the probable exception of the passion account, which appears to give an almost day by day account of events, the Gospel is made up of a number of isolated stories, which have no connection with each other. The earliest Christians therefore did not write a narrative of Jesus' life but preserved and made use of individual units or short passages about Jesus' words and deeds. The details about the time and place, when and where events happened, are not an essential part of the original story.

Only for the last half century have scholars treated the gospel writers as authors. Prior to that time they were commonly regarded as compilers, that is, individuals who in somewhat random fashion simply placed the stories about Jesus found in the oral tradition alongside one another. If we look at Mark as an author, we discover his own vocabulary and style, and his own themes. While being bound somewhat by the tradition he received, he appears to have been free to tell the story in a way that would have brought out for Christians in his community the significance of Jesus some forty years after his death.

It was the author we refer to as Mark, therefore, who shaped the narrative by his use of sources, his own theological convictions, concerns, and interests, and those of his intended audience. Mark is not concerned to present academic history, rather he is writing preached history. He wants to convince his audience that Jesus fulfilled

God's promises to Israel. He is concerned with presenting the story of someone he believes is the Son of God. It is this conviction that governs his presentation of the Jesus story.

Jesus according to Mark's Gospel

What, then, does Mark emphasize in his presentation of Jesus' career? It is usually noted that the framework of this Gospel is partly geographical and partly christological. The story begins with Jesus' activity in Galilee (1:14–9:49), then mentions how he set out from there and passed through the area "across the Jordan" (10:1), through Jericho (10:46-52), and on to Jerusalem (11:1–16:8). Only rarely does Jesus go into Gentile territory (5:1-20; 7:24-37), but those who acknowledge him there and the centurion who confesses Jesus at the foot of the cross (15:39) foreshadow the gospel's expansion into the Gentile world. The first half of the narrative takes place in Galilee and adjacent areas of northern Palestine, a largely rural area of peasant farmers where Jesus recruits his followers, performs numerous miracles and—despite some opposition—enjoys considerable success. The second half relates Jesus' fatal journey southward to Judea and Jerusalem, where he is rejected and killed.

Tied to this theme is the progressive revelation of Jesus' identity as Son of God. Mark is very interested in his readers' understanding of who Jesus is. We will see that misunderstanding the identity of Jesus leads to misunderstanding discipleship. Because Mark wrote his Gospel for followers and potential followers of Jesus, it is not surprising that the question of Jesus' identity (christology) is one of his major themes. Mark has Jesus himself raise this question when he asks his disciples, "Who do you say that I am?" (8:29).

The three principal titles Mark uses for Jesus are "Son of God," "Son of Man," and "Messiah" (Christ). These titles serve to identify Jesus as the anointed descendant of David promised in the Old Testament, a mighty figure who is to come with power and glory on the clouds of heaven, and one who has a special relationship to God and is obedient to God's will. As the story unfolds, it becomes clear that Jesus is also one who is destined to suffer, die, and be raised from the dead. In fact, we misunderstand who Jesus is if we ignore his humiliation, suffering, death, and resurrection.

For Mark, the point of emphasis in the life of Jesus is naturally its end on the cross, which is the culmination of his suffering. This is why almost half of Mark, from 8:27 onward, is overshadowed by the passion of Jesus. The Gospel ends, however, not with the cross but in the resurrection. Throughout his Gospel, Mark has looked beyond the passion both to a resurrection after three days and to a second coming of Jesus as Son of Man. In the last chapter, there is the story of Mary Magdalene and Mary, the mother of James and Salome, going to anoint Jesus in the tomb and not finding him there. Jesus was risen. Throughout the Gospel, Mark links Jesus' suffering with his resurrection. Mark's audience would have understood the message as it pertained to them. Jesus' path to glory and eternal life included suffering. Similarly, the Markan community, which was undergoing persecution in the late first century, would have understood that their current suffering was a necessary prelude to glorification.

18

The main christological titles Mark uses for Jesus (Son of God, Son of Man, Messiah) are important, but in attempting to answer the crucial question of Jesus' identity, one must not focus on these exclusively. Very early in the Gospel the reader is introduced to Jesus as one who proclaims "the gospel of God" (1:14). The content of this proclamation is included in the next verse: "This is the time of fulfillment. The kingdom of God is at hand. Repent, and believe in the gospel" (1:15). Mark stresses Jesus' message about the kingdom of God now breaking into human life as good news (1:14-15). The Christian is now free from the value system of the world, free to be influenced by God's will as manifested in the teaching of Jesus.

The reader soon learns that Jesus is more than merely the messenger who announces the inbreaking of God's reign with its reversal of human values. Mark presents Jesus as exercising great authority during his ministry. As a teacher he taught with a note of authority (1:21-22). He rejects much of the tradition of Judaism (7:1-13) and seems to contravene the written Law (7:14-20). Jesus exercises authority over the sabbath (2:27-28) and over the temple. In chapter 11, he seems to take command of the temple and asserts his authority over its customs. Jesus alone knows the secret of the kingdom of God (4:10-11), has the authority to forgive sins (2:5-12), and authority over nature (4:35-41; 6:45-52).

Jesus did many powerful deeds during his ministry. He exercises "authority" and is a miracle worker. Mark is thus suggesting that one not concentrate only on the words of Jesus; his deeds are important as well. These marvelous deeds need to be explained, however. Otherwise, such acts of power are ambiguous and subject to misinterpretation.

The authority of Jesus, the hiddenness and suffering aspect of his messiahship are key themes in Mark. The reader also learns that the one who announces the inbreaking of the kingdom of God has come to serve, not to be served (10:45).

Mark's Gospel and Christianity Today

Mark invites us to reflect on these themes and on the importance of Jesus in our own lives at the beginning of the twenty-first century. In the chapters that follow, we will examine Mark's presentation of the Jesus story in an effort to understand how this Gospel might be of use to us today. It is my hope that the comments made and the questions raised will help the modern reader to engage in a meaningful dialogue with this ancient text. Mark's Gospel has been of enormous import in the history of Christianity; may this book help to make it an important text for you in your personal and communal journey of faith.

I

The Miracle-Working Son of God Who Will Be Put to Death

(1:1 – 3:6)

Mark begins his story of Jesus in a way that Christians unfamiliar with this Gospel usually find rather strange. There is no infancy story; no shepherds and no magi appear in the initial part of this Gospel. The section which we will examine in this chapter begins with the identification of Jesus as the Son of God and ends with the stunning news that the Pharisees and Herodians are planning to put Jesus to death (3:6).

Introduction (1:1-13)

¹ The beginning of the gospel of Jesus Christ (the Son of God). ² As it is written in Isaiah the prophet: "Behold, I am sending my messenger ahead of you; he will prepare your way. ³ A voice of one crying out in the desert: 'Prepare the way of the Lord, make straight his paths.'" ⁴ John (the) Baptist appeared in the desert proclaiming a baptism of repentance for the forgiveness of sins. ⁵ People of the whole Judean countryside and all the inhabitants of Jerusalem were going out to him and were being baptized by him in the Jordan River as they acknowledged their sins. ⁶ John was clothed in camel's hair, with a leather belt around his waist. He fed on locusts and wild honey. ⁷ And this is what he proclaimed:

"One mightier than I is coming after me. I am not worthy to stoop and loosen the thongs of his sandals. 8 I have baptized you with water; he will baptize you with the holy Spirit." 9 It happened in those days that Jesus came from Nazareth of Galilee and was baptized in the Jordan by John. 10 On coming up out of the water he saw the heavens being torn open and the Spirit, like a dove, descending upon him. 11 And a voice came from the heavens, "You are my beloved Son; with you I am well pleased." 12 At once the Spirit drove him out into the desert, 13 and he remained in the desert for forty days, tempted by Satan. He was among wild beasts, and the angels ministered to him.

The first thirteen verses of chapter 1 are usually seen as an introduction to the Gospel. The modern reader does not need to pay too much attention to the chapter and verse divisions, since these do not appear in the earliest manuscripts. The Gospel was divided into chapters only in the thirteenth and into verses in the sixteenth century.

In any case, 1:1-13 contains events which must happen before Jesus can embark on his public ministry. They designate the mission and message of John the Baptist, report the baptism and temptation of Jesus, and lead up to the arrest of John in 1:14. Mark has no birth narrative or genealogy; he tells us nothing of the background or descent of Jesus. In 1:9 we learn that Jesus came from Nazareth in Galilee. This is as much as Mark knows or pretends to know.

Christ, the Son of God

Although the reader does not meet him until 1:9, Jesus' importance for Mark and his Gospel can be seen earlier. In the first verse, in fact, Jesus is identified as the "Son of God." While this part of the verse may have been added by a later editor, since it is not present in all early manuscripts, it does draw the reader's attention immediately to the issue of christology. Most modern research has pointed to the fact that a major reason for the writing of Mark's Gospel was a christological problem. A correct understanding of Jesus is therefore crucial for Mark. But what does "Christ the Son of God" mean for Mark? His entire Gospel deals with this question, answering it with a narration of Jesus' words and deeds.

What would "Christ" and "Son of God" have meant to Mark's original audience? The term "Christ" comes from a Greek word, which means "anointed" and is a translation of a Hebrew word with the same meaning. The English terms "Christ" and "Messiah," therefore, are words which refer to an "anointed" person.

We need to keep in mind that at Jesus' time there was no unanimously agreed upon Jewish doctrine of the Messiah. In the Hebrew Scriptures the term "anointed" is used of Israelite kings (Saul, David, and David's successors), a non-Israelite king (Cyrus of Persia), priests (Aaron and his sons), prophets (Elisha) and the Servant of the Lord (Is 61:1-2). In certain periods of Israelite history there was a vivid hope that a new era would begin under the leadership of an anointed son of David. After the Babylonian exile (587-38 B.C.E.), however, the priestly rulers of Israel, rather than the Davidic king, became the focal point of such future hopes. The Dead Sea Scrolls reveal that at Qumran (ca. 140 B.C.E. to 68 C.E.) there was the expectation of two messiahs, one priestly and one political. Most scholars conclude that the general Jewish expectation at the time of Jesus was for a political king and military leader, who would drive out the Romans.

In the first verse of his Gospel, Mark appears to use "Christ" as both a personal name and a title for Jesus. In fact, by the time of Mark's writing, this title had become so closely associated with Jesus that it came to be used almost as a second name. Mark is thus expressing here a fundamental Christian claim: Although he did not closely resemble the political/military leader expected by Israel, Jesus was the Messiah, the Savior God had promised to Israel. And the early Christian community viewed the resurrection of Jesus as God's confirmation of this.

The story of Jesus of course begins well before Mark's Gospel. The Christian tradition is really the Judeo-Christian tradition. Messiah, the title that early Christians associated most closely with Jesus, is a title found in the Hebrew Scriptures. Mark and his contemporaries were able to find many scriptural references that, correctly understood, pointed to just the type of Messiah that Jesus was. Thus, Mark guides his readers to a Christian understanding of the Hebrew Scriptures.

In a similar way, while God speaks to each individual through the words of scripture, we too need a trustworthy guide to insure our correct understanding of the text. Such insight may be gained from a number of places (e.g., a homily, a study guide, a Bible-sharing group). Oftentimes, however, the word of God is only understood after considerable meditation. We therefore should make use of helpful commentaries, as long as our focus is on the word of God, which the secondary text strives to illuminate.

For reflection: The Old Testament texts were written

down many years before Jesus conducted his ministry. But when we look at the Hebrew Bible through the prism of Jesus and his career, we see some of these texts in a different light. Similarly, events in our own lives can cause us to discover meaning in a text that we had not noticed in earlier readings. Therefore, one reading of the Gospel is not enough. As our situation in life changes we need to revisit Mark's story of Jesus. New insights into God, Jesus and God's will for us will shine forth when we encounter God's word anew.

Mark invites us to look again at the person of Jesus. This is the focus of his entire Gospel. In 1:7-8, for example, the first words of John the Baptist concern one who is to come: He immediately directs our attention to Jesus. While Mark concentrates upon Jesus' words and deeds, his interest is in proclaiming who Jesus *is,* not just who he was. Mark is not merely interested in relating a story from the past but wants to tell his audience why Jesus, the risen Lord, is important for their daily lives. Similarly, we too should ask ourselves: What does it mean for me to say that Jesus is the Messiah? Is Jesus important for my daily life?

While Mark believes that Jesus is the Jewish Messiah (correctly understood), his most important title for Jesus is "Son of God." How does Mark understand this title? Today, we can too easily misinterpret Mark's meaning. As a result of reading Homer's *Iliad,* or other works of Greek mythology, some arrive at the mistaken conclusion that Jesus became the Son of God as the result of a physical begetting. Although this view is not usually held by Christians, some people will see little difference between the Christian claim that Jesus is both the "Son of God" and the "Son of Mary" (6:3) and Homer's story in which Achilles is both the son of the sea goddess Thetis and the mortal man Peleus. The Semitic background of the title "Son of God" makes this interpretation impossible. For God to have intercourse with a female consort or a human being would have been repugnant to the Hebrew faith.

After the formal declarations of the Council of Nicea (325 C.E.), Christians have been tempted to interpret "Son of God" by using terms like "being" and "substance," which are derived from Greek metaphysics. This metaphysical understanding dates to a time later than the Gospel of Mark, however, and is the result of reflection on biblical texts in light of Greek philosophy. While this philosophical language might be helpful for Christians today as they reflect on the person of Jesus, this would not have been Mark's frame of mind. In order to understand what Mark had in mind when he used this term to refer to Jesus, we should examine the use of this title in the Hebrew Scriptures. References to "Son of God" in the Old Testament denote a moral and functional relationship, not a metaphysical one. The title means being chosen or elected to a task, thus participating in the work of God; it implies obedience, the obedience of a son to a father. This functional understanding thus has priority over the metaphysical one. For Mark, to be the Son of God means to be obedient to God's will.

For reflection: Almost two thousand years later, we need to reflect on the person of Jesus and take him as a model for our own behavior. We should look at Jesus' relationship to God as presented in Mark's Gospel and understood in the Christian tradition. Just as the Son of God is obedient to God's will, so must those he calls brother, sister, and mother be obedient to God's will.

The title "Son of God," appears again in the first chapter when the voice from heaven speaks at Jesus' baptism (1:11). Here, Mark has someone other than himself declare Jesus to be the Son of God. This messianic royal title would have been familiar to Mark's readers from the cult of emperor worship and from the Hebrew Scriptures. The king was addressed as the son of god at an annual celebration. Jesus is thus being installed forever as the universal king. In the Hebrew Scriptures this term is used for the nation of Israel (Ex 4:22; Hos 11:1), for the king as the leader and symbol of the nation (2 Sam 7:14), and for other figures who receive some special commission from God (e.g., ministering angels in Dn 3:25, 28).

This important declaration is communicated only to Jesus; no witnesses are mentioned. Mark 1:10 says "he saw"; Jesus alone saw. And the voice addresses only Jesus when it says "you are." God, the voice from heaven, speaks directly to Jesus, who alone sees the Spirit. These verses are part of what scholars call the "Messianic secret." In Mark's Gospel, Jesus' identity is not known during his career. He cannot be recognized prior to his passion. To understand Jesus correctly, we must realize that suffering and death are crucial components of Mark's definition of Messiahship.

Jesus is declared Son of God at the beginning, middle, and end of the Gospel. On each of these occasions the statement is accompanied by supernatural or cosmic signs. In the baptism and transfiguration stories a voice from heaven proclaims Jesus as God's beloved Son

(Mk 1:11; 9:7). At the foot of the cross the centurion confesses that Jesus is the Son of God (15:39). In a somewhat similar vein there are the utterances of his enemies, the cry of the demons (3:11f.; 5:7), and the question of the high priest at the trial before the Sanhedrin (14:61f.). The voice from heaven only speaks twice in the Gospel, and both times it identifies Jesus as the Son of God. The demons know who Jesus is; they have a correct understanding of him. His disciples, on the other hand, never refer to Jesus as the Son of God.

Why would our author tell the story in this fashion? The two most popular answers to this question are not mutually exclusive. In Mark, as in the other New Testament writings, the good news is preached first to the Jews and then to the Gentiles. Christianity is something different from Judaism; it is not a subdivision of Judaism. This means that one does not need to become a Jew in order to become a Christian. Some scholars suggest that with this story, Mark wants to point to the fact that the Jewish people and the Jewish disciples of Jesus misunderstand him, whereas the Roman soldier, the Gentile centurion, correctly understands that Jesus is the Son of God.

For reflection: Those who should have recognized, understood and accepted Jesus, those who were the heirs to the religion of the patriarchs and most familiar with its contents, were the ones who rejected him. The ones who did accept him instead were the Gentiles, non-Jews. This should lead any Christian familiar with the biblical texts to thoughtful contemplation and humble reflection. Is it similarly possible that my understanding of the biblical texts is farther from the correct conclusion than that of a non-Christian reader? It would seem unlikely, but the biblical material itself urges us to be cautious about our assumptions.

A second answer concerning why Mark would tell the story of Jesus in this manner is that the *timing* of the centurion's confession is the key, rather than the fact that he was a Gentile. Jesus is not identified as the Son of God by a human being when he performs powerful deeds or issues authoritative teachings. Only when he is hanging on the cross in humiliation and death is he recognized for who he is.

Mark's message to his original audience resounds throughout the centuries: If your understanding of Jesus does not include his suffering and death, you have misunderstood him. This picture of Jesus has obvious ramifications for discipleship according to Mark. The disciple should expect no better treatment than the master received. Therefore, as we lead our lives of service following the example of Jesus, we too might have to suffer and even die as a result of carrying out God's will.

As we will see below, Mark's message is that the end time has already begun with the career of the earthly Jesus. Armed with the power of the Spirit, the Son of God speaks with authority and vanquishes the demons. Yet his authority and victory can only be discerned in the light of the cross. This is the climax of his mission, for he came not to be served but to serve and to offer his life for all (10:45).

Repent and Believe (1:14-15)

   [14] After John had been arrested, Jesus came to Galilee proclaiming the gospel of God: [15] "This is the time of ful-

fillment. The kingdom of God is at hand. Repent, and believe in the gospel."

Mark 1:14 is a transitional verse in which the reader learns about John's arrest and Jesus' appearance in Galilee. The stage is now set for Jesus to speak for the first time in this Gospel. When he does so, he states that the period in human history appointed by God for the fulfillment of his messianic promises has arrived. The time is fulfilled, the reign of God is here. What is called for is repentance and faith.

Israel's long wait for God to fulfill his promises has come to an end. Jesus affirms that today a new time has begun. Jewish apocalyptic eschatology thought in terms of two ages. These were distinct: One age ended and the other began by an intervening act of God. According to Mark, the coming of Jesus is this act. Christians are no longer under the sway and influence of the present evil age. They are now free to conduct their lives in accordance with the values of the reign of God. Jesus has come to reconcile us to God and to one another. Christians are free to direct their whole being toward the other, to serve as Jesus served. All they need to do is to repent and to believe in Jesus, the Messiah, the Son of God.

Mark presents Jesus' call to repent and believe in the gospel as the appropriate response to Jesus' announcement of the arrival of God's reign, part of Jesus' basic message addressed to all those who heard his preaching. What Jesus is calling for is a radical and unconditional conversion from all that is evil and a total commitment to God. The positive side of this complete commitment to God's will is faith.

What one understands to be the content of the "gospel" or "good news" depends on where one stands in time. The Galilean audience that Jesus is pictured as addressing in Mark 1:15 would have understood this to include, at least, Jesus' news that the reign of God was at hand and, probably also, his teaching concerning God's will (i.e., how one ought to conduct one's life now that the reign of God had arrived). The original readers or hearers of Mark's Gospel, living some forty years after Jesus' ministry, would undoubtedly have seen this "good news" as including the early Christian preaching about Jesus, the Christ. The messenger has thus become the message. The acceptance of the message of and about Jesus follows from the complete turnabout in life that Jesus demands. Individuals can submit to God's will by following the way of Jesus, which includes leading one's life in accordance with the values of the reign of God and participating in the new type of human community made possible by its arrival.

Call of the First Disciples (1:16-20)

> [16] As he passed by the Sea of Galilee, he saw Simon and his brother Andrew casting their nets into the sea; they were fishermen. [17] Jesus said to them, "Come after me, and I will make you fishers of men." [18] Then they abandoned their nets and followed him. [19] He walked along a little farther and saw James, the son of Zebedee, and his brother John. They too were in a boat mending their nets. [20] Then he called them. So they left their father Zebedee in the boat along with the hired men and followed him.

Jesus' general call for conversion and belief (1:15) leads immediately to his much more particularized call of the first disciples. The call to repentance and faith focuses on the kingdom/reign of God as the content of the good news; the invitation to follow him focuses on personal attachment to the person of Jesus. The first words of Jesus to his disciples are thus a call to commit themselves to him.

Jesus calls his first disciples as he is walking along the shore of the Sea of Galilee. They respond by leaving their place of work and following him. Jesus continues what John began. People are uprooted; they break with their vocation and family. The nucleus of the kingdom of God is founded by getting people on the way and following Jesus.

The initiative in this call story, as later in the call of Levi (2:14), is taken by Jesus. These fishermen, whom Jesus encountered as he made his way along the shore of the Sea of Galilee, were not seeking to join him. In fact, they do not appear to have been seeking anything. When Jesus met them they were simply engaged in tasks which were considered part of their occupations, casting or mending their fishing nets. Similarly, when Jesus came to call Levi, he found Levi busy with his duties as a tax collector.

God seems to address his call to ordinary people as they go about their daily lives. This invitation is not something one earns, but it comes freely from God. Throughout the Bible, God chooses to work through specific individuals and groups (e.g., Israel, the Church) to accomplish God's purposes. The timing of God's call and the state of the person chosen often appear puzzling to the reader. Why choose a crafty deceitful twin (Jacob), the son of a slave (Moses), a prostitute (Rahab), or a widow from Moab (Ruth)?

Men and women, usually seen as unlikely candidates by

the reader, are chosen by God, not because they are already holier than others, but in the hope that they will cooperate with God for the successful accomplishment of God's will. This call of the first disciples highlights the gratuitous and unexpected nature of God's call and the response required from the one called.

Many of the above-mentioned examples are not specifically ones of a Christian faith. Members of other faiths also believe in God and his protection. Christian faith starts instead when we take seriously Jesus' call to follow *him,* and when we change our way of life according to his teachings. What is needed is to trust Jesus as one's personal guide in life.

For reflection: In the earliest days of Jesus' ministry, the call to follow him actually did mean leaving friends, family and occupation in order to accompany him during his travels. As time has gone on, it has come to mean putting Jesus and the doing of God's will first and foremost in one's life. This might involve a change of residence, a different career path, and new friends, but it does not necessarily have to include these. It is likely, however, that there will be changes in one's life, and that some of these changes will be unsettling. With this in mind it is easy to see how the message of Jesus continues to challenge individuals. Am I too comfortable with much of my life as it is now? Am I ready to experience anxiety when I realize that following Jesus more closely will require changes in my life? Am I prepared to commit myself to following what I know to be the correct path when it will likely be painful and costly?

First Miracle Stories (1:21-45)

> [21] Then they came to Capernaum, and on the sabbath he entered the synagogue and taught. [22] The people were astonished at his teaching, for he taught them as one having authority and not as the scribes. [23] In their synagogue was a man with an unclean spirit; [24] he cried out, "What have you to do with us, Jesus of Nazareth? Have you come to destroy us? I know who you are—the Holy One of God!" [25] Jesus rebuked him and said, "Quiet! Come out of him!" [26] The unclean spirit convulsed him and with a loud cry came out of him. [27] All were amazed and asked one another, "What is this? A new teaching with authority. He commands even the unclean spirits and they obey him." [28] His fame spread everywhere throughout the whole region of Galilee.

Jesus' first public act after gathering his disciples is an exorcism that takes place in the synagogue at Capernaum, where the community gathered each sabbath for the chanting of the psalms and the reading of the Bible. It is in this setting that Jesus reveals himself as one with authority. In reaction to his teaching an unclean spirit screams. Jesus' mission involves the overthrow of the demonic power structure. Satan was overcome in the temptation scene (1:12-13), and now his henchmen have been defeated.

Of all the miracle stories available to him, Mark chose to place first the miracle which interpreted Jesus' teaching as sharing the power of his mighty acts (1:21-28). Why bracket this story of the cure of a demoniac with verses that speak of Jesus as a teacher? Numerous times in the Gospel, Mark uses a technique known as intercalation (also called, sandwich technique, bookends, or brackets).

This is a technique whereby an author surrounds a section with two similar stories/verses. In such a case, the end pieces help one interpret what is between them, and the center has something to do with the brackets. In the story concerning the demoniac, Mark tells us that the power at work in Jesus was, and is, at work also in his words.

29 On leaving the synagogue he entered the house of Simon and Andrew with James and John. 30 Simon's mother-in-law lay sick with a fever. They immediately told him about her. 31 He approached, grasped her hand, and helped her up. Then the fever left her and she waited on them. 32 When it was evening, after sunset, they brought to him all who were ill or possessed by demons. 33 The whole town was gathered at the door. 34 He cured many who were sick with various diseases, and he drove out many demons, not permitting them to speak because they knew him. 35 Rising very early before dawn, he left and went off to a deserted place, where he prayed. 36 Simon and those who were with him pursued him 37 and on finding him said, "Everyone is looking for you." 38 He told them, "Let us go on to the nearby villages that I may preach there also. For this purpose have I come." 39 So he went into their synagogues, preaching and driving out demons throughout the whole of Galilee. 40 A leper came to him (and kneeling down) begged him and said, "If you wish, you can make me clean." 41 Moved with pity, he stretched out his hand, touched him, and said to him, "I do will it. Be made clean." 42 The leprosy left him immediately, and he was made clean. 43 Then, warning him sternly, he dismissed him at once. 44 Then he said to him, "See that you tell no one anything, but go, show yourself to the priest and offer for your cleansing what Moses prescribed; that will be proof for them." 45 The man went away and began to publicize the whole matter. He spread the report abroad so that it

was impossible for Jesus to enter a town openly. He remained outside in deserted places, and people kept coming to him from everywhere.

By the time we get to the end of chapter 1, it is clear that exorcisms and healings are the two principal approaches that Jesus uses to translate the kingdom of God into action. In both, Jesus intrudes upon enemy territory. He challenges and defeats the forces of evil that stand in the way of the fulfillment of the kingdom.

These healing stories point out to us that even though the kingdom is here, it is in a state of conflict; there is an element of completeness to be reached only in the future, and therefore we need to have faith. Mark seems to describe a world in which there is some degree of tension. He and his readers live in the "already but not yet." He believes that something has changed with the coming of Jesus into the world; the world is full of new possibilities. But we have not yet arrived at the end of history. Christians can still sin; evil is still a powerful force in the world.

There have been some Christians throughout history who have taken a triumphalistic attitude toward life in this world. In their eyes Jesus came to bring the gift of eternal salvation; we have received the promise of this gift and there is nothing we can do to lose it. People with this attitude experience little tension in their lives. They pretend to live at the end of history with no more surprises. This often results in a rather cavalier attitude toward sin and evil. No matter what I do, it cannot possibly affect my eternal salvation. This attitude also questions why anyone would suffer for their faith. Since eternal salvation is guaranteed, why experience this needless pain? This attitude seems to ignore one of the basic themes of Mark's Gospel:

We are not yet at the end of history; Christians still need to repent and believe.

For reflection: The healing stories in Mark's Gospel point to the fact that a Christian participates in the reign of God insofar as he or she fights evil in the world. Evil, whether mental, physical or moral, has no place in the reign of God. In working to rid the world of sickness and disease we are therefore cooperating with God's will.

Just as demonic possession and illnesses of varying types are visible signs in Mark's Gospel that the reign of God is not here in its fullness, the curse of poverty and homelessness are indications that all is not well in the human community today. As we look at the world in which we live, there are certain signs that the reign of God has not yet come in its fullness. Too many individuals and nations are motivated by the all-consuming desire for profit and the thirst for power, imposing their will upon others. There is a lack of human solidarity, an absence of basic justice, and little respect for human rights. Considering the world of today, it is appropriate to include moral sickness in this list. Evil can also operate in such a way that people do not feel it, causing them to be blinded or confused about the truth. The power of Jesus is active wherever individuals are working to shape a society that better protects the dignity and basic rights of their brothers and sisters and wherever people are helping those who are spiritually and morally blind to see the truth.

Ambiguities about Miracle Stories and Opposition to Jesus (2:1-12)

As Mark begins the next section of his story (2:1–3:6) he does not say that Jesus continues to exorcize and heal. Something new is added: conflict. Jesus is challenged both in what he says and in what he does.

Mark, more than the other evangelists, devotes a great proportion of his Gospel to miracle stories. He obviously conceived of Jesus as one who performed such acts of power, and Mark seems to see these as part of Jesus' struggle against the forces of evil. It is in exorcisms that Jesus shows his mastery over Satan and provides evidence that he acts by the power of God.

But what does a miracle prove about the one who performs it? Does it prove that Jesus is God's promised, anointed one, who is involved in the inbreaking of God's visible rule in the world?

The Hellenistic world was full of wonder workers and magicians. The miracle stories in Mark's Gospel are very similar in form to Hellenistic stories about mighty miracle workers. There are also Jewish texts in which rabbis heal the sick, overcome evil spirits, cause rain to start and stop, and so on. And the god Asclepius was said to cause the lame to walk, the blind to see, and to be able to heal the disfigured. That similar stories were told about Jesus did not set him apart from his age, they made him quite at home in it.

Nobody will deny that Jesus had powers which enabled him to heal those who were plagued by evil spirits. According to Mark, his contemporaries had no doubt that such powers were miraculous. But in Mark's Gospel, almost all of these stories carry some interpretation. Mark is not concerned to glorify Jesus as just one wonder worker among others, whose exploits excel the rest. He is the Holy One of God (1:24), the Son of God (3:11), and the "stronger one," who binds the strong man (Satan) and wrests his prey from him (3:27). These stories portray the strong compassion of Jesus for the oppressed, the outcast, those whom society has condemned as unclean, the lepers and the demoniacs.

With his preaching of the kingdom, Jesus himself is the messenger of good news (1:14f.). He delivers authoritative teaching and opposes the piety of legalistic Judaism. He consorts with sinners and calls *them,* not the righteous, to the joy of repentance. But no less is he victorious over the power of Satan and the forces of disease and illness. Jesus shows himself to be the promised Messiah by both his words and deeds.

While many today believe that these mighty acts of power prove all sorts of things about Jesus, we must be careful to look at the evidence in Mark's Gospel before jumping to conclusions. A careful reading of this Gospel indicates that Jesus' miracles might be evidence of God's power but could be misunderstood as simply being magic tricks. In Mark 3 one reads that the scribes thought Jesus cast out demons by the power of Beelzebul (3:22). The friends and relatives of Jesus thought him to be crazy, out of his mind (3:21). The Pharisees witnessed many of the miracles of Jesus, but apparently thought them so inadequate that they had to ask for a special demonstration or sign from Jesus. Even Jesus' disciples seem to miss the point of the miracles. They participated in the two feeding stories, yet were unable to make sense of them (8:17-18).

Since it is unclear what exactly miracles prove about the

miracle worker, it would have been easier for the early Church simply to forget Jesus' mighty deeds and to concentrate on him as a thinker and teacher. Why hand on a tradition that is ambiguous at best, and at worst makes Jesus out to be another wandering magician? The answer is that, while the miracles were as much a problem in the first century as they are today, Jesus really did perform such powerful acts as part of his ministry. Rather than ignore Jesus' miracles, therefore, Mark chose to reinterpret them by placing them in a specific context or, as we shall see below, by adding an introduction or conclusion. These would typically focus on the power Jesus exercised during his ministry and often suggest an application to the situation of the reader of Mark's Gospel.

¹ When Jesus returned to Capernaum after some days, it became known that he was at home. ² Many gathered together so that there was no longer room for them, not even around the door, and he preached the word to them. ³ They came bringing to him a paralytic carried by four men. ⁴ Unable to get near Jesus because of the crowd, they opened up the roof above him. After they had broken through, they let down the mat on which the paralytic was lying. ⁵ When Jesus saw their faith, he said to the paralytic, "Child, your sins are forgiven." ⁶ Now some of the scribes were sitting there asking themselves, ⁷ "Why does this man speak that way? He is blaspheming. Who but God alone can forgive sins?" ⁸ Jesus immediately knew in his mind what they were thinking to themselves, so he said, "Why are you thinking such things in your hearts? ⁹ Which is easier, to say to the paralytic, 'Your sins are forgiven,' or to say, 'Rise, pick up your mat and walk'? ¹⁰ But that you may know that the Son of Man has authority to forgive sins on earth"— ¹¹ he said to the paralytic, "I say to you,

rise, pick up your mat, and go home." [12] He rose, picked up his mat at once, and went away in the sight of everyone. They were all astounded and glorified God, saying, "We have never seen anything like this."

The above healing story is the most obvious interpreted miracle. The story begins as a debate about Jesus' ability to heal the physical problems of this man. It soon becomes clear, however, that the real question is whether Jesus can forgive sins. This is an important question for us who, like the reader of Mark's Gospel some forty years after Jesus' death, can no longer benefit directly from the physical presence of the healing Jesus. The message of this Gospel story is that the same power that allows Jesus to heal also allows him to forgive sins. And the reader of Mark's Gospel does have access to this power.

Stories that told of Jesus' mighty deeds were shaped to show that the power which could perform such wonders during Jesus' career was still present for those who, through faith in him, became members of the Church. Jesus was the risen Lord, who continued to be with his people.

For a Christian, Jesus' deeds are not the exploits of any ordinary miracle worker. They may have been intended originally as immediate and direct epiphanies of the divine wonder worker, but Mark intervened to connect them with Jesus' message of salvation. In order to understand the miracles of Jesus in Mark you have to understand who Jesus is. And according to Mark this is possible only when one considers his ultimate fate, death on the cross and resurrection.

41

Jesus Breaks with Traditional Customs (2:13–3:6)

¹³ Once again he went out along the sea. All the crowd came to him and he taught them. ¹⁴ As he passed by, he saw Levi, son of Alphaeus, sitting at the customs post. He said to him, "Follow me." And he got up and followed him. ¹⁵ While he was at table in his house, many tax collectors and sinners sat with Jesus and his disciples; for there were many who followed him. ¹⁶ Some scribes who were Pharisees saw that he was eating with sinners and tax collectors and said to his disciples, "Why does he eat with tax collectors and sinners?" ¹⁷ Jesus heard this and said to them (that), "Those who are well do not need a physician, but the sick do. I did not come to call the righteous but sinners."

The stories of the call of Levi (2:13-14) and the table fellowship with sinners (2:15-17) indicate that the reign of God is inclusive, not exclusive. In traditional Jewish piety one avoided what was unclean. It was as if sin was a contagious illness. To associate with sinners would have negative effects on your stance before God. Jesus instead calls and eats with those who were traditionally excluded. He goes into the world and touches impurity, knowing that these are the very people who need him the most.

For reflection: These stories invite us to reflect on our own actions. To live in the reign of God we will have to change some of our values. How do we relate to the outcasts of society? Do we talk about the human dignity of prostitutes, drug addicts, and convicted criminals, yet refuse to treat them like human beings? Do we talk about the plight of the jobless and homeless, yet never take steps to assist them? Do we only love those who love us?

42

During the time of Jesus, Israel was under the domination of the Roman Empire. The tax collectors were Jews who worked for the Romans, people who served a foreign power. A symbol of Roman oppression, they were considered traitors and/or thieves by many. Jesus however does not ignore such people; he seeks them out. Similarly, if we want to be his followers, we too must liberate ourselves from prejudice and discrimination.

> [18] The disciples of John and of the Pharisees were accustomed to fast. People came to him and objected, "Why do the disciples of John and the disciples of the Pharisees fast, but your disciples do not fast?" [19] Jesus answered them, "Can the wedding guests fast while the bridegroom is with them? As long as they have the bridegroom with them they cannot fast. [20] But the days will come when the bridegroom is taken away from them, and then they will fast on that day. [21] No one sews a piece of unshrunken cloth on an old cloak. If he does, its fullness pulls away, the new from the old, and the tear gets worse. [22] Likewise, no one pours new wine into old wineskins. Otherwise, the wine will burst the skins, and both the wine and the skins are ruined. Rather, new wine is poured into fresh wineskins."

In this third controversy story, Jesus overturns the traditional days of fasting and substitutes a new fast day. Fasting is a sign of penance and repentance; it was seen to support the people in their prayers that God would come and liberate them. When Jesus is present, however, joy and celebration are more appropriate than fasting. A new calendar is created, a new time. The community that calls Jesus Lord and Savior has broken away and cannot adjust to the old ways. Instead of fasting twice a week as the Jews did, Jesus suggested a fast on the anniversary of his death. Jesus endorses the weekday of his death as a day of fasting and thus dissociates the Markan people from the old order of fasting.

For reflection: Are our attitudes and actions joyful and celebrative? Do we conduct our lives as people of hope and confidence? Are we afraid of things that are new and different? Are we reluctant to change? Not everything old is bad, and not everything new is good. But we should walk through life with joyful confidence in Jesus and his promise of eternal salvation. Since Jesus called for repentance (1:15) with his first words in this Gospel, we can conclude that there are appropriate times for fasting even today. Most Christians observe portions of the season of Lent, especially Holy Week, as an appropriate time for penance and fasting.

In a Gospel that emphasizes the suffering of Jesus as much as Mark does, it is easy to conclude that Christians should stress Good Friday. But this is also a Gospel that presents Jesus as Son of God and the one who fulfilled the promise of the resurrection. We should not focus on Good Friday to the extent that the joy of Easter Sunday is lost or forgotten.

This text also suggests that the Christian calendar is different from the secular one. The Christian should, for example, see beyond the commercialism of Christmas. And true followers of Jesus know that there is more to the celebration of Easter than the Easter bunny. Community worship is important, and one day a week is set aside for this. Many Christians celebrate All Saints' Day, All Souls' Day and a variety of other special days. None of these days is usually given special attention in the secular world, where one day is just like another. Mark invites us to review the calendar that governs our own lives. Is our calendar today different from that of the surrounding secular culture?

> 23 As he was passing through a field of grain on the sabbath, his disciples began to make a path while picking the heads of grain. 24 At this the Pharisees said to him, "Look, why are they doing what is unlawful on the sabbath?" 25 He said to them, "Have you never read what David did when he was in need and he and his companions were hungry? 26 How he went into the house of God when Abiathar was high priest and ate the bread of offering that only the priests could lawfully eat, and shared it with his companions?" 27 Then he said to them, "The sabbath was made for man, not man for the sabbath. 28 That is why the Son of Man is lord even of the sabbath." 3:1 Again he entered the synagogue. There was a man there who had a withered hand. 2 They watched him closely to see if he would cure him on the sabbath so that they might accuse him. 3 He said to the man with the withered hand, "Come up here before us." 4 Then he said to them, "Is it lawful to do good on the sabbath rather than to do evil, to save life rather than to destroy it?" But they remained silent. 5 Looking around at them with anger and grieved at their hardness of heart, he said to the man, "Stretch out your hand." He stretched it out and his hand was restored. 6 The Pharisees went out and immediately took counsel with the Herodians against him to put him to death.

These two sabbath stories end this section and lead to the death plot (3:6). Mark tells us that Jesus is free to do as he pleases on the sabbath, as are his followers. Jesus can act in this way because of the inherent importance of his

45

person. And Christians are permitted to continue the work of the kingdom on the sabbath.

As Jesus talks of saving life, his opponents plan to take his. The controversy stories culminate in a death plot against Jesus. His fate is sealed from early in the ministry, not because he announces the kingdom of God, but because he does so in direct opposition to the religious order of the day.

For reflection: Thus we are invited to be self-critical, as individuals and as a community of faith. We must examine our own religious tradition in light of the scriptures and from our contemporary vantage point. Some elements of the tradition have a permanent value; others, only a transitory one. We must be careful to understand the difference. The changeable circumstances in which we find ourselves invite us to listen carefully to inquiring minds and to encourage constructive insights. But Mark tells us that following in the footsteps of Jesus means that we must also be ready to suffer for preaching and teaching the truth.

II

Opposition and Mystery
(3:7 – 4:34)

After the first open threat on his life, Jesus withdraws to the lake in 3:7. What follows at first is an undisturbed period of exorcizing and healing. In 3:9, Jesus asks for a boat, which he uses for his speech in chapter 4 and to go across the lake after the speech. These trips back and forth across the lake are a significant structural characteristic of the following section of Mark's Gospel, as will be seen in our next chapter. In this chapter we will examine Mark's presentation of the opposition to Jesus, which solidifies prior to Jesus' first major speech in this Gospel. Then we will comment on the speech itself.

Jesus Followed by Large Crowds (3:7-12)

⁷ Jesus withdrew toward the sea with his disciples. A large number of people (followed) from Galilee and from Judea. ⁸ Hearing what he was doing, a large number of people came to him also from Jerusalem, from Idumea, from beyond the Jordan, and from the neighborhood of Tyre and Sidon. ⁹ He told his disciples to have a boat ready for him because of the crowd, so that they would not crush him. ¹⁰ He had cured many and, as a result, those who had diseases were pressing upon him to touch him. ¹¹ And whenever unclean spirits saw him they would fall down before him and shout, "You are

the Son of God." [12] He warned them sternly not to make him known.

Mark begins this section of the Gospel by informing the reader that large crowds from many different regions were coming to see Jesus. Through his teaching and his powerful deeds Jesus was able to draw many to himself. Later in the text, the masses who respond positively to Jesus are contrasted again with the small groups that reject him (Mk 3:20-30).

The initial attraction of people from a variety of different places foreshadows the influx of Gentiles into the Christian community after the resurrection. It also brings to our attention a challenge, which was present at the time of the early Christians and which we are still facing today. When the gospel is carried from one culture to another, previous ways of understanding, of learning, and of teaching are challenged. What was assumed as essential to the gospel message in one culture is often seen as disposable in another. Jesus had proclaimed the gospel message in Aramaic with illustrations from the village and rural life of Galilee; Mark was writing in Greek to a mixed community of Jews and pagans, who may have spent their lives in the urban environment of a Roman metropolis. This transition exposed all the purely Jewish assumptions in which the gospel had previously been clothed. Jewish cultural and religious forms were recognized as not an essential element of the gospel.

For reflection: This can serve to remind us today that Christianity is a worldwide religion. Many people from different countries are attracted to Jesus. People today hear about his words and deeds and decide to investigate

48

for themselves. How often do we identify as essential to the gospel message things which other cultures see as dispensable? It is good to remind ourselves that just as "Christian" is not a synonym for Jew or Gentile, neither is it a synonym for Roman or European. A Christian is a believer in the risen Jesus, and Christians can be found in a variety of different cultures. Diversity characterized the Church's very beginnings; the unifying factor was, and is, one's basic attitude toward Jesus of Nazareth.

"Being With" Jesus (3:13-19)

> [13] He went up the mountain and summoned those whom he wanted and they came to him. [14] He appointed twelve (whom he also named apostles) that they might be with him and he might send them forth to preach [15] and to have authority to drive out demons: [16] (he appointed the twelve:) Simon, whom he named Peter; [17] James, son of Zebedee, and John the brother of James, whom he named Boanerges, that is, sons of thunder; [18] Andrew, Philip, Bartholomew, Matthew, Thomas, James the son of Alphaeus; Thaddeus, Simon the Cananean, [19] and Judas Iscariot who betrayed him.

Mark informs us that Jesus called the twelve together after he went up a mountain. In the Judeo-Christian biblical tradition mountains serve as special places. In Mark's Gospel several important acts take place on mountains: the call of the twelve (3:13ff.), Jesus at prayer(6:46), the transfiguration (9:2ff.), and the apocalyptic discourse of chapter 13. A mountain is therefore an ideal place for revelation in religious literature. Although we do not conduct our daily lives in a three-tiered universe where heaven is "up," it is still common to find individuals or groups who feel closer to God when on a mountain top. God can, of course, be experienced in other natural settings (e.g., deserts, the sea, forests), or for that matter, in any setting. But mountains have a natural religious significance in that they seem to bring us closer to the transcendent.

According to Mark, Jesus ascended a mountain to call the twelve to "be with him" (3:14) and to "send them forth to preach and to have authority to drive out demons" (3:14-15). Mark never says explicitly what "being with" Jesus means; rather he shows it to us throughout his Gospel. At the very least, being with Jesus involves seeing his works and hearing his words. In addition to this physical understanding of being with Jesus, there also seems to be an interior attachment of fidelity that is required. The call to become a companion of Jesus, an associate in ministry, suggests something more than mere physical presence. In this case, we see that this call also includes a missionary responsibility.

For reflection: We saw earlier that the call to follow Jesus is a call to conversion of life, to obedience, trust and hope. Many Christians today agree also that the missionary enterprise is an important part of discipleship, yet assign it to others within the Church. Is mission a personal or a collective responsibility? In Mark's Gospel many individuals other than the twelve proclaim the good news. How can we as individual Christians and local communities fulfill this missionary charge in our own lives? Do we need to preach the good news of God's salvation publicly in foreign lands? In our own community? Or can we fulfill this requirement simply by following the example of Jesus and leading a life of humble service?

50

Opposition to Jesus (3:20-30)

[20] He came home. Again (the) crowd gathered, making it impossible for them even to eat. [21] When his relatives heard of this they set out to seize him, for they said, "He is out of his mind." [22] The scribes who had come from Jerusalem said, "He is possessed by Beelzebul," and "By the prince of demons he drives out demons." [23] Summoning them, he began to speak to them in parables, "How can Satan drive out Satan? [24] If a kingdom is divided against itself, that kingdom cannot stand. [25] And if a house is divided against itself, that house will not be able to stand. [26] And if Satan has risen up against himself and is divided, he cannot stand; that is the end of him. [27] But no one can enter a strong man's house to plunder his property unless he first ties up the strong man. Then he can plunder his house. [28] Amen, I say to you, all sins and all blasphemies that people utter will be forgiven them. [29] But whoever blasphemes against the Holy Spirit will never have forgiveness, but is guilty of an everlasting sin." [30] For they had said, "He has an unclean spirit."

small literary unit

In the final two pericopes of chapter 3, the contrast between those who follow Jesus and those who do not is emphasized. The opposition to Jesus solidifies prior to his speech in chapter 4. Jesus' family declares him to be out of his mind or mentally deranged, and the scribes assert that he works miracles by the power of Beelzebul. The sense of opposition is highlighted by Mark's use of the technique of intercalation. By bracketing the objections of the scribes (3:22-30) with the comments of Jesus' relatives (3:20-21, 31-35), Mark indicates that the attitude of Jesus' family toward him is similar to that of the scribes. Thus, those who should have recognized the importance of Jesus misunderstand him. In response to his family and the scribes, we find Jesus gathering a new family around him.

For reflection: There is good evidence that the members of Jesus' family were not among his followers prior to the resurrection (cf. Jn 7:5). Do we who claim to be followers of Jesus recognize his importance and conduct our lives according to his teachings? Or are we more like his natural family and the scribes, suggesting by our actions that we actually reject his teachings?

In this section, Mark also presents Jesus as one who drives out demons. The question concerns the source of Jesus' power to cast them out. The options seem clear: Either Jesus casts out demons by the power of the Holy Spirit or he does so by the power of Satan. Those who attribute Jesus' power to Satan, the source of evil, seem to be putting limits on the power of God. This, then, would be the "everlasting sin" (3:29), which cannot be forgiven.

Is there any modern equivalent to the claim that Satan, and not the Holy Spirit, was at work in Jesus? We might think of Satanic cults and devil worship, which are on the rise in certain parts of our world. It is one thing to be unconvinced by the Christian claims for Jesus. It is quite another to claim that Jesus was able to exorcize and heal only because he was possessed by Satan. However, rather than focusing on the "everlasting sin," it would be much more in keeping with the gospel message to emphasize the overwhelming grace of God, which forgives "all sins and all blasphemies that people utter" (3:28).

Communitarian Aspects of Discipleship (3:31-35)

[31] His mother and his brothers arrived. Standing outside they sent word to him and called him. [32] A crowd seated around him told him, "Your mother and your brothers (and your sisters) are outside asking for you." [33] But he said to them in reply, "Who are my mother and (my) brothers?" [34] And looking around at those seated in the circle he said, "Here are my mother and my brothers. [35] (For) whoever does the will of God is my brother and sister and mother."

These verses, in which Jesus defines what it means to be a member of his family, are some of the more important ones in this section of the Gospel. For Mark, discipleship means, in fact, joining Jesus' new family. In the new community established by his proclamation of God's reign, Jesus' natural family has no real importance. He makes it clear that "whoever does the will of God" is his brother, sister and mother, and has thus fulfilled the requirement for membership in his eschatological family.

To be a Christian, it is not enough merely to be attracted to Jesus. We must come to believe that Jesus is the Christ, the Son of God. This belief necessarily leads us to conduct our lives according to the teachings of Jesus. What is required is more than merely *pondering* the mystery of God's salvation. Words without acts are empty. The new family of Jesus is made up of those who *do* God's will (3:35). We will see more about this later.

This passage also brings to light that from the start Christianity was a communitarian movement. There is, of course, a vertical dimension to discipleship. The relationship between the individual and Jesus is very important. However, this focus on the vertical dimension, the individual's own personal call and subsequent relationship with the Lord, should not lead to selfishness and a lack of concern for others. Christian discipleship is more than just a private, internal matter. There is an essential horizontal dimension to it as well. When Jesus identifies those who do God's will as his mother, brothers, and sisters, it is implicit that these disciples are also related to one another.

The household or family is one of the basic images of Christian social identity and cohesion. In the ancient world, the extended family was the source of one's status in the community and functioned as the primary economic, religious, educational and social network. If we recognize the communal nature of Christianity, best expressed by this image of the family, we will realize that other followers of Jesus are our brothers and sisters. Most people find it much harder to ignore the needs of a friend or relative than those of a stranger. Therefore, if we start to see the other members of the Christian community as our brothers and sisters in Christ, we will feel a greater responsibility for their welfare.

For reflection: Does the realization that we are all brothers and sisters lead us, as members of this new community, to adopt an unselfish, sharing lifestyle? Does it result in more active involvement in and commitment to the community and its members? If not, then does the problem lie in the fact that we do not really accept the fact that we are members of Jesus' new family?

Emerging Church Structures

Mark also implies that within this new family of Jesus there is the need for some kind of structure. It is not accidental that Mark places the mission of the twelve immediately after the section on the great number of people who are attracted to Jesus. Prior to this pericope we have heard of the call of Simon and Andrew, James and John (1:16-20), and been told that Levi left his customs post and followed Jesus (2:13-17). Now, due to the large numbers of people attracted to Jesus, there is need of more structure among his disciples. From among his followers, Jesus chose twelve to be with him in a special way. These he commissioned to go forth and preach. He also gave them the authority to drive out demons. The mission of Jesus is thus extended to a wider audience by means of these early missionaries. They do what he does. It is a short step from this realization to the conclusion that the Church carries on the ministry of Jesus in word and deed.

Once we recognize the importance of the communal dimension of discipleship for Mark, we must examine his Gospel in an effort to see what it tells us about the structure of this early Christian community.

What we find in Mark's Gospel is very little structural differentiation. Everyone seems to do everything without much status distinction. There is a functional distinction between Jesus and his followers, but very little evidence of functional specialization among these followers. The twelve are singled out from among the larger group of disciples to "be with" Jesus "that he might send them forth to preach and to have authority to drive out demons" (13:14-15). But also others in this Gospel are with Jesus, preach, and cast out demons. Among the twelve there is some rudimentary role specialization when Peter, James, and John (and sometimes Andrew) are singled out from among the larger group of Jesus' followers to witness the raising of Jairus' daughter (5:37) and the Transfiguration (9:2-9), to ask the question which leads to the apocalyptic discourse (13:3-4), and to go off with Jesus while he prays in Gethsemane (14:32ff.). Generally speaking, however, the twelve and/or the disciples act together as a homogeneous unit, all of them able to perform a variety of functions.

The disciples of Jesus are seen debating their internal power and status on two occasions in Mark's Gospel (9:33-37; 10:41-45). In the first instance Jesus places a child in their midst and talks to them about being servants of all. After the next argument, Jesus tells the disciples that the Gentiles exercise authority over each other, but that such activity is forbidden among them. In spite of this apparent prohibition against vertical differentiation (the unequal power and influence attached to various roles resulting in a status hierarchy), the prominent role of Peter in the Gospel suggests that it always was present beneath the surface.

The almost egalitarian nature of the community in Mark's Gospel is seen especially in Jesus' words on how the Gentiles rule: "You know that those who are recognized as rulers over the Gentiles lord it over them, and their great ones make their authority over them felt. But it shall not be so among you. Rather, whoever wishes to be great among you will be your servant; whoever wishes to be first among you will be the slave of all" (10:42-25). Instead of power and the exercise of authority, Jesus emphasizes service.

56

Mark's picture of the original followers of Jesus, as loosely organized and almost without structure, invites us to reflect on our own experience of the Church. It is true that there is no uniform order or structure to the Church of the New Testament; it varied from place to place. However, there is some order and structure, which shapes the life and mission of the early Church. The Christian community grows and develops as it journeys through the centuries. We must show a sensitivity about both the validity and the limitations of the past as well as an openness to the present and the future. The Church of the first century grew and developed into the Church of the second century, which, in turn, grew and developed into the Church of the third century, and so on. We should be open to the possibility of change. Some past decisions will be viewed as normative, yet others will be seen as inappropriate or incomplete understandings of God's will for the present. This raises the possibility of new Church structures and new models of leadership in the Church.

For reflection: Would the almost egalitarian Church structure suggested in Mark's Gospel be the best way for the modern Christian community to be organized? Should we cast off the accretions of almost two thousand years and try to create a loosely structured Church? Or should we adopt the growth and development model and conclude that the Church structure we experience today is the logical and necessary outcome of two millenniums of existence? Are the hierarchy and structure of your church the result of refinement that has taken place over time and is needed for the people of God to flourish at this time in history?

Jesus' First Major Discourse (4:1-12)

The stage is now set for Jesus' first major speech in this Gospel. He has spoken about our need to do God's will in order to be considered one of his relatives. In this speech he will suggest that one's actions in this life have eternal consequences. It is a speech in which Jesus tells his followers about the hostile world in which they live and the need to have hope and faith in God's ultimate control over history.

> 4:1 On another occasion he began to teach by the sea. A very large crowd gathered around him so that he got into a boat on the sea and sat down. And the whole crowd was beside the sea on land. 2 And he taught them at length in parables, and in the course of his instruction he said to them, 3 "Hear this! A sower went out to sow. 4 And as he sowed, some seed fell on the path, and the birds came and ate it up. 5 Other seed fell on rocky ground where it had little soil. It sprang up at once because the soil was not deep. 6 And when the sun rose, it was scorched and it withered for lack of roots. 7 Some seed fell among thorns, and the thorns grew up and choked it and it produced no grain. 8 And some seed fell on rich soil and produced fruit. It came up and grew and yielded thirty, sixty, and a hundredfold." 9 He added, "Whoever has ears to hear ought to hear."

This is the first of two speeches of Jesus in Mark's Gospel (the other extended discourse is found in chapter 13). Here we see a pattern that is found elsewhere in Mark. Jesus first teaches publicly to the crowd and the disciples in parables, and then instructs his disciples again in private (4:1-12; 7:14-23; 9:14-29; 10:1-10; 13:1-8). The point is that the disciples of Jesus had a greater opportunity to understand what Jesus said and did. Yet they do not seem to profit from it (cf. 6:52; 8:21; 9:32) and later desert him.

This theme—providing someone with excellent opportunities to understand is no guarantee of understanding or of faithful behavior—is prevalent in the Bible as well as in ordinary daily life. The Hebrew Bible is replete with stories of how the people of the covenant violated their agreement with God. God usually responded by sending them leaders or prophets to call them back. All too often, however, the result was continued violation of the covenant. Similarly, most people have friends or relatives, who are no longer practicing Christians despite growing up in worshiping Christian families and being well educated religiously. Many people who are afforded the opportunity to understand about Jesus and God's will for us do not seem to profit from this instruction. This theme will appear again in Jesus' discourse (see below).

Regarding the disciples in Mark, it is interesting to note that while they are portrayed badly, it was with these followers that the tradition about the words and deeds of Jesus began. If they misunderstood so badly, how can Mark use those traditions with any confidence? Perhaps the reader is meant to conclude that at some point (more hinted at than stated) they finally did come to understand. Later readers of the gospel can learn a lesson from this. It takes time to know Jesus completely. Often misunderstanding is the earliest response.

Before commenting on any particular pericope, we need to discuss the fact that Jesus is presented as teaching to the crowd in parables. What are parables and why does Jesus choose this genre to communicate his message about the inbreaking kingdom of God?

The English word "parable" is a transliteration of the Greek *parabole,* which in turn translates the Hebrew *mashal.* In the Hebrew Bible, proverbs, riddles and sentences of the wise are all called *meshalim* (plural of *mashal*). Both Jesus and the rabbinic tradition contain *meshalim* like those in the Hebrew Bible, but they also contain a genre not found there. It is this genre, a short narrative fiction used to reference a symbol, which we call a parable. In Jesus' parables the symbol referenced is the kingdom of God. A parable, then, is a story about familiar things that seeks to get the listener to perceive something new in his or her situation. It is usually drawn from nature or everyday life, startles the hearer because of its vividness or strangeness, and is sufficiently puzzling to tease the mind into active thought. It is the point of the story as a whole that is important, not every detail of it.

> [10] And when he was alone, those present along with the Twelve questioned him about the parables. [11] He answered them, "The mystery of the kingdom of God has been granted to you. But to those outside everything comes in parables, [12] so that 'they may look and see but not perceive, and hear and listen but not understand, in order that they may not be converted and be forgiven.' "

Mark locates the majority of Jesus' parables in chapter 4, where the so-called hardening theory appears. Jesus informs his disciples that the mystery of the kingdom of God has been granted to them while to those outside this group everything comes in parables (4:11-12). The reason given is contained in the citation of Isaiah 6:9 (4:12).

Evidence from the Hebrew Bible concerning the *mashal*

suggests that a parable is not a simple, clearly understandable story. Interpretation is an inherent aspect of *mashal,* and misunderstanding is an inevitable risk. Those who can interpret the parable are on the inside, followers of Jesus; but for those outside all things are insoluble riddles.

The usual reading of this text is not to conclude that Jesus taught in parables in order to confuse people and prevent them from being converted. Most readers recognize that the reaction to Jesus presented throughout Mark's Gospel is the typical reaction people give to the prophetic call to return to God: Some respond positively while others reject the call. The one who recognizes Jesus as the Son of God and the herald of the kingdom and follows him understands the parables. Those who do not recognize or follow Jesus fail to understand anything about him and are confused by the parables. This passage is thus best understood as describing the predicted result of Jesus' teaching in parables rather than its purpose.

In the modern world stories about what Jesus said and did still cause confusion. Those Christians who have faith are usually characterized by their quest for understanding. This is often a difficult task. One studies the text, reflects on it, and seeks help in searching for an adequate or appropriate understanding. To those outside the Christian faith community, the meaning of these passages often remains obscure. The reason for this confusion, in many cases, seems to be a lack of understanding concerning the person of Jesus. Those who do not recognize Jesus as the herald of the kingdom of God, the one in whose words and deeds God is at work, are not able to understand what he says and does.

The Kingdom of God as Mystery (4:13-20)

[13] Jesus said to them, "Do you not understand this parable? Then how will you understand any of the parables? [14] The sower sows the word. [15] These are the ones on the path where the word is sown. As soon as they hear, Satan comes at once and takes away the word sown in them. [16] And these are the ones sown on rocky ground who, when they hear the word, receive it at once with joy. [17] But they have no root; they last only for a time. Then when tribulation or persecution comes because of the word, they quickly fall away. [18] Those sown among thorns are another sort. They are the people who hear the word, [19] but worldly anxiety, the lure of riches, and the craving for other things intrude and choke the word, and it bears no fruit. [20] But those sown on rich soil are the ones who hear the word and accept it and bear fruit thirty and sixty and a hundred-fold."

In 4:11, the first word in this speech that Jesus addresses to his disciples, this exclusive circle of insiders, reveals that they are being entrusted with the mystery of the kingdom of God. With this introduction the reader expects a mystery to be revealed, but none is. Mark tells the story in such a way that the reader has to find out what the mystery is, and thus be counted among the insiders. By definition, the listener must be actively involved in seeking a correct understanding of a parable and thus of God's kingdom; and so it is with the reader of Jesus' speech in Mark 4.

In this five-part speech, Jesus speaks about the mystery of the kingdom of God. But what is it that is being revealed? What is this mystery? It has long been noted that several of the stories that make up this speech contain a contrast between beginnings and endings. The interpretation of the Parable of the Sower (4:13-20) is the first of these so-called growth parables. In spite of the traditional title for this parable, the focus is not on the sower but on the seeds and what happens to them.

As we saw in the first words of Jesus (1:15), the reign of God exists here and now in the present; the word has been sown in God's offer of the kingdom in the preaching of Jesus. The present experience of the Markan community (and our own), however, is not what one would have expected. God's offer has not been embraced enthusiastically and accepted with gratitude; instead, it has provoked mixed reactions. Some of the seeds fail to take root, some germinate but do not grow, some germinate and grow but fail to make it to harvest. Jesus' preaching results in different reactions, and some fall away because of persecution or worldly temptations. This is no reason for despair; failure is inevitable in sowing.

In this pericope Jesus speaks about a threefold failure and then a threefold success. The parable's structure leads to the expectation of abundant growth as a metaphor of God's mighty activity. This becomes clear when we realize that normal yields are between two- and fivefold. The impossible yield in this parable is an example of hyperbole. There will be tribulation and persecution but ultimate victory. This parable serves as a source of encouragement to those facing opposition. The reign of God goes through phases; one must have faith.

For reflection: As mentioned above, our situation today is, in many ways, similar to that facing the Markan community. The word of God is being preached in a world that remains hostile to it. Some are initially attracted to the Christian message, but fall away when they realize that following Jesus will place some serious demands on them. Others are seduced by the promises of riches and pleasure. Jesus' interpretation of this parable makes clear the dangers of wealth. Sometimes the word of God, which enters a person like a seed, is unfruitful in the end. While hearing the word of God is very important, it is in vain if it does not lead to producing fruit (cf. 3:35). In many ways life in this world is more challenging for those who choose to follow Jesus. As friends, relatives, neighbors, or co-workers seem to be flourishing outside the Christian community do we envy them? Or do we really believe that we possess something important that is missing from their lives?

The Future Coming of the Kingdom (4:21-25)

> 21 He said to them, "Is a lamp brought in to be placed under a bushel basket or under a bed, and not to be placed on a lampstand? 22 For there is nothing hidden except to be made visible; nothing is secret except to come to light. 23 Anyone who has ears to hear ought to hear." 24 He also told them, "Take care what you hear. The measure with which you measure will be measured out to you, and still more will be given to you. 25 To the one who has, more will be given; from the one who has not, even what he has will be taken away."

As we have seen, Jesus and the kingdom appear but are now misunderstood by many. Because the kingdom has not come yet in its fullness and because Jesus is unrecognized by most of his contemporaries, Mark can speak about the hiddenness of Jesus and the kingdom. But the parable of the lamp tells us that what is hidden now will become manifest in the future (4:22). The apparent insignificance of Jesus' earthly ministry will be vindicated by the glorious coming of the kingdom. Insignificant though the earthly Jesus may appear, he is the beginning of God's final glorious rule.

For reflection: The modern reader of this pericope, like other readers throughout the centuries, stands between the first and second coming of Christ. In this in-between time we are asked to have faith. We are told that the kingdom has come in the person of Jesus yet it remains hidden for the present. It will be revealed in all its glory in the future. Do you believe this? Is your life sustained by faith in Jesus as the Son of God and hope in his promised return and the coming of the kingdom in its fullness?

The so-called measure saying (4:24-25), which appears next, indicates that conditions will intensify, for better or worse. The one who has will get more and the one who has not will have what he or she has taken away. These verses have two popular interpretations. If we relate them to 4:10-12, the citation of Isaiah 6, then we can conclude that a similar message is found in the measure saying. Those who already have some spiritual insight, presumably the followers of Jesus, will have this increased by exposure to Jesus' parables. Those who do not, will end up in greater spiritual ignorance.

Others have taken the measure saying to be referring to final judgment. Those who accept the present, yet hidden, reality of the kingdom of God, and conduct their lives in accordance with this invisible kingdom and Jesus' teachings, will receive their reward at final judgment. Those who instead fail to accept the present reality of the kingdom, and do not conduct their lives accordingly, will lose whatever they have at final judgment.

These interpretations are not mutually exclusive. A correct understanding of Jesus will lead to greater spiritual insight when one hears his parables. This, in turn, should lead to a clearer understanding of God's will and to a life lived according to the teachings of Jesus. Such active faith will be rewarded at final judgment. For those who do not see Jesus as the Son of God and the bringer of the kingdom, exposure to his parables results in more confusion. These individuals will not have a clear understanding of God's will and will not receive a reward at final judgment.

Growth of the Kingdom (4:26-29)

> [26] He said, "This is how it is with the kingdom of God; it is as if a man were to scatter seed on the land [27] and would sleep and rise night and day and the seed would sprout and grow, he knows not how. [28] Of its own accord the land yields fruit, first the blade, then the ear, then the full grain in the ear. [29] And when the grain is ripe, he wields the sickle at once, for the harvest has come."

The seed growing secretly is the second so-called growth parable in chapter 4. The contrast is again between the smallness of the seed and the final harvest. The fact that the seed sprouts and grows "of its own accord" (4:28), without the farmer's help, suggests both the mysterious nature of what is happening and the inevitability of the process. Once it is set in motion the kingdom pursues its course toward fulfillment.

It is important to remember here that we are dealing

with a parable, not an allegory. In an allegory, every element stands for something else. Those who would read this as an allegory are tempted to see Jesus as the man who scatters the seed. This, in fact, is not necessary and would be a mistake. Remember, in a parable it is the point of the story as a whole that is important, not every detail of it.

The point of this parable is that God is guiding the process. God is in charge of the timetable for the growth and development of the kingdom and its coming in fullness, even though this might not be apparent. This parable serves to encourage those living at a time in between sowing and harvest. What is now hidden will be revealed in glory.

The Mustard Seed (4:30-34)

> [30] He said, "To what shall we compare the kingdom of God, or what parable can we use for it? [31] It is like a mustard seed that, when it is sown in the ground, is the smallest of all the seeds on the earth. [32] But once it is sown, it springs up and becomes the largest of plants and puts forth large branches, so that the birds of the sky can dwell in its shade." [33] With many such parables he spoke the word to them as they were able to understand it. [34] Without parables he did not speak to them, but to his own disciples he explained everything in private.

The last of the three growth parables in this section of the Gospel is the pericope that ends this discourse. The parable of the mustard seed (4:30-32) serves to articulate well the main point of the speech. The minuteness of the seed and the magnitude of the full grown shrub are contrasted. The kingdom in miniature will become the kingdom which covers the entire land. The present and invisible reign of God will become gloriously manifest in its universal dimensions. This provides consolation and hope to people who see only despair in the present. The reign of God is under heavy attack from Satan and the forces of evil, but the seed has been sown and in time will develop fully.

The eschatological tree of Ezekiel 17 and 31 and Daniel 4 undoubtedly has influenced the transmission of this parable. In these texts from the Hebrew Bible the tree is the mighty cedar of Lebanon. The cedar suggests strength and protection but is also a symbol of arrogance and pride. In Mark's Gospel the mustard bush is seen as a more suitable metaphor for the kingdom of God than the cedar. This is reminiscent of the contrast between the Messiah, expected to be a political king or military leader who would violently overthrow the Roman government, and Jesus, the humble, suffering Messiah.

This parable, like those which precede it, causes the reader to think seriously about Jesus and his message and warns against judging by appearances. By speaking in parables, Jesus engaged his audience in thinking about the ways of God and the coming of the kingdom in a way that he would not have been able to had he used plain speech.

According to most commentators, the present experience of the Markan community involved persecution and suffering. The Christian message was not being embraced enthusiastically by all, and many had left the community because of worldly anxiety and the lure of riches. Mark's claim, however, is that faith is called for because God is ultimately in control of events.

For reflection: Our present situation is not unlike that of the Markan community. The kingdom has not come in its fullness; many who were enthusiastic initially have left the Church. Some have fallen away because of suffering or persecution, others have been lured away by earthly wealth. In this situation we are asked to have faith in Jesus as the bringer of the kingdom, and to model our lives on his. We are told that the grace of God allows us the possibility of living human life in the way God wanted us to lead it. Do we live with hope in the future coming of the kingdom in its fullness? Do we recognize Jesus as the herald of God's coming kingdom so as to understand present situations correctly?

III

Jesus' Northern Ministry:
Jews and Gentiles
(4:35 – 8:21)

The fact that in 4:35–8:21 Jesus continually travels back and forth across the Sea of Galilee has interested readers of Mark's Gospel for many years. It is clear that Mark does not present Jesus as an aimless wanderer but as someone with a definite purpose and goal. So what is Mark's teaching about Jesus and his message in this section of the Gospel?

A clue is found in this section's final pericope (8:14-21), in which Mark highlights the importance of understanding. At the end of his northern ministry, Jesus and his disciples set out in a boat to cross the Sea of Galilee. During this crossing, Jesus castigates his followers for their lack of comprehension and offers them some hints, which, one assumes, should lead them to a proper understanding of his ministry thus far. Jesus first asks his disciples how many baskets full of fragments they picked up after he fed the five thousand. After they answer his question, he asks them how many full baskets of fragments they picked up after the feeding of the four thousand. Jesus responds to their answer by asking them, "Do you still not understand?" (8:21). But what is it that Jesus wants them to understand?

Most readers wonder why Mark has included two

stories about Jesus feeding the multitudes (6:30-44; 8:1-10). This interest is heightened when one realizes that Jesus summarizes his entire northern ministry by asking his disciples to recall specific details from the two feeding stories. In addition, after each multiplication story the reader is informed that the disciples failed to understand about the loaves.

A solution to this puzzle begins to emerge when we focus on both the multiplication stories and the boat trips across the Sea of Galilee. Mark is using Jesus' travels around Galilee and its environs to symbolically reflect the unity in God's kingdom of Jew (west of the Sea) and Gentile (east of the Sea and northwards). The fact that the two feeding stories take place on opposite sides of the Sea of Galilee suggests that in this section of the Gospel Mark sees Jesus as a great unifier, someone who is inaugurating God's kingdom on the Gentile side of the lake as well as on the Jewish side.

This conclusion is supported by other similarities between what happens on the western and on the eastern side of the Sea of Galilee. The first miracle that Jesus performs in the Gospel is the exorcism in Capernaum (1:21-28) on the Jewish side of the lake. This is immediately followed by his healing of Peter's mother-in-law (1:29-31). The same pattern—exorcism followed by healing—takes place on the eastern or Gentile side of the lake: Jesus crosses the lake for the first time after his kingdom of God speech in chapter 4. When Jesus and his disciples arrive at the country of the Gerasenes, Jesus exorcizes the unclean spirits from the demoniac (5:1-20). After performing this exorcism, Jesus and his followers return to the Jewish side of the lake. Immediately after their second trip to the Gentile side of the lake, Jesus begins to heal the sick people who are brought to him (6:53-56), as he had healed Peter's mother-in-law.

What message was Mark trying to deliver to his original readers by telling the story in this way? How can the recognition that Mark has arranged many disparate stories from the tradition in this manner help us in our own spiritual journey?

Jesus was born and raised a Jew; his initial followers were all Jews. Their belief about Jesus would have set these first disciples of Jesus apart from other Jewish groups, but in many other ways they would have looked much like just another Jewish sect. In the beginning, therefore, there would have been no reason to question the Jewishness of this group. And there is good evidence that once it *was* questioned, instead of vanishing, it turned into an explicit assertion. Even some twenty years after the death of Jesus, Jewish Christian missionaries were trying to insist that one had to be a Jew, or at least that one had to observe certain Jewish practices, in order to be a Christian (cf. Gal 2; Acts 15).

The community to which Mark wrote was probably a mixed community of Jews and Gentiles. Perhaps the relationship between Christianity and Judaism was still an issue in the community, or perhaps there were memories, however distant, of these earlier clashes over the identity of the Jesus movement. In any case, by telling the story of Jesus in the fashion he did, Mark has found support in the ministry of Jesus for the reality which Christianity came to be. And he has also done so in a marvelously subtle way.

Jesus is not presented as stating clearly and unambiguously that Gentiles could become members of the kingdom of God without becoming Jews. He is shown to have delivered this message in a more mysterious, parabolic fashion, and it is easy to understand how Jesus' original followers might have missed the point. By extension, of course, it is not surprising that some in the Christian community continued to miss this point for several decades. Mark has continued the method he began in chapter 4. The believer, the reader, must be actively engaged in questioning and trying to understand God's will.

Christians today face similar issues. In talking about how God communicates through the gospel, we cannot disregard the influence of the community in which we live. Cultures shape human life and development.

For reflection: We too need to ask ourselves: What is God's will with respect to the issues of variety and unity? When is diversity constructive and when is it destructive? For example, are different weekend worship services in English, French, Spanish and Vietnamese positive for a community? Is it essential that the members of such a community have a common worship experience from time to time?

How do you react when there is an attempt to unite different elements in the community into something new? Does the mixture of traditional organ music and guitars playing folk songs make for a more meaningful liturgical celebration? What is your response to change? What did you say to your friends when someone younger, or of a different race or nationality, or of a different gender, assumed a leadership role in your faith community?

Having set out the general structure of this section of the Gospel, let us now take a look at some of the pericopes which Mark used in his construction of 4:35–8:21. Keeping Mark's overall goal for this section in mind, we will examine selected passages in an effort to understand how they might raise questions that would be spiritually significant for us today. First, we will examine 4:35–6:6, which culminates in Jesus' rejection in Galilee by his own townspeople. Then, we will comment on 6:7–8:21, where Jesus begins his final journey and is rejected beyond Galilee.

The Storm on the Sea (4:35-41)

[35] On that day, as evening drew on, he said to them, "Let us cross to the other side." [36] Leaving the crowd, they took him with them in the boat just as he was. And other boats were with him. [37] A violent squall came up and waves were breaking over the boat, so that it was already filling up. [38] Jesus was in the stern, asleep on a cushion. They woke him and said to him, "Teacher, do you not care that we are perishing?" [39] He woke up, rebuked the wind, and said to the sea, "Quiet! Be still!" The wind ceased and there was great calm. [40] Then he asked them, "Why are you terrified? Do you not yet have faith?" [41] They were filled with great awe and said to one another, "Who then is this whom even wind and sea obey?"

During their trip across the lake, the disciples woke Jesus but did not call upon him to use his power to rescue them from the dangers of the raging sea. This suggests that they did not recognize Jesus' ability to perform miracles, and that they had no faith in Jesus as the one who could save them. They simply appear puzzled at Jesus' lack of concern about their predicament (4:38). Once awake, Jesus performs a powerful miracle in his stilling of the storm (4:39). The overall reaction of the disciples leads Jesus to ask them, "Do you not yet have faith?" (4:40).

In this story the disciples refer to Jesus as "teacher" (4:38), as they do in two other miracle stories (cf. 5:35; 9:17). Mark sees Jesus as the teacher par excellence, whose person, words and deeds become the content of Christian teaching. Much of Jesus' teaching about the coming of God's kingdom, or about behavior that is appropriate for those who await it, is easily comprehended. As we have seen, however, other stories and sayings of Jesus are cryptic, challenging the hearers to puzzle over their meaning. In almost every case, Mark has provided the reader with the help needed to understand the pericope.

The picture of Jesus sleeping during the storm suggests his confidence in God—a confidence his disciples are lacking. Mark also suggests that Jesus is doing things which in the Hebrew Scriptures were reserved to God. There are many stories in the Ancient Near East in which the sea or a sea monster appears as a symbol of chaos and evil that struggles against God. The Israelites were aware of these stories and of the suggestion that creation resulted when God subdued the sea monster (referred to as "Rahab" or "Leviathan"). In calming the sea, Jesus therefore does what God did in the Hebrew Scriptures. God's power is now at work in Jesus. The use of the present tense of "obey" has been seen by some to indicate that Jesus' power still operates in Mark's church. With the disciples' question in 4:41, "Who then is this?" the focus remains on the person of Jesus. As with the interpretations he provides to the miracle stories, here too Mark wants to alert his readers to Jesus' continued presence and activity in their midst.

Later in the tradition, when the Church had come to be symbolized as the bark or ship of Peter, preachers used this pericope to suggest that Christ would continue to care for his Church.

For reflection: Is there any evidence that Jesus is present today among his followers? Do you believe that Jesus cares about the difficulties you face and is willing and able to intervene on your behalf? Are you able to react calmly in the midst of certain crises because you believe that ultimately God is in control of events?

The Gerasene Demoniac (5:1-20)

5:1 They came to the other side of the sea, to the territory of the Gerasenes. 2 When he got out of the boat, at once a man from the tombs who had an unclean spirit met him. 3 The man had been dwelling among the tombs, and no one could restrain him any longer, even with a chain. 4 In fact, he had frequently been bound with shackles and chains, but the chains had been pulled apart by him and the shackles smashed, and no one was strong enough to subdue him. 5 Night and day among the tombs and on the hillsides he was always crying out and bruising himself with stones. 6 Catching sight of Jesus from a distance, he ran up and prostrated himself before him, 7 crying out in a loud voice, "What have you to do with me, Jesus, Son of the Most High God? I adjure you by God, do not torment me!" 8 (He had been saying to him, "Unclean spirit, come out of the man!") 9 He asked him, "What is your name?" He replied, "Legion is my name. There are many of us."

[10] And he pleaded earnestly with him not to drive them away from that territory. [11] Now a large herd of swine was feeding there on the hillside. [12] And they pleaded with him, "Send us into the swine. Let us enter them." [13] And he let them, and the unclean spirits came out and entered the swine. The herd of about two thousand rushed down a steep bank into the sea, where they were drowned. [14] The swineherds ran away and reported the incident in the town and throughout the countryside. And people came out to see what had happened. [15] As they approached Jesus, they caught sight of the man who had been possessed by Legion, sitting there clothed and in his right mind. And they were seized with fear. [16] Those who witnessed the incident explained to them what had happened to the possessed man and to the swine. [17] Then they began to beg him to leave their district. [18] As he was getting into the boat, the man who had been possessed pleaded to remain with him. [19] But he would not permit him but told him instead, "Go home to your family and announce to them all that the Lord in his pity has done for you." [20] Then the man went off and began to proclaim in the Decapolis what Jesus had done for him; and all were amazed.

After Jesus calms the sea, he and his disciples arrive safely on the Gentile side of the lake. Jesus' first act upon arriving on the eastern side of the Sea of Galilee is the healing of the Gerasene demoniac, Jesus' most massive exorcism in Mark. In the stilling of the storm, Jesus has just shown his tremendous power over nature. In this pericope he demonstrates his power in the case of possession. This exorcism parallels Jesus' first act on the Jewish side of the lake, the exorcism reported in 1:23ff. Jesus has come to free the Gentiles from demonic uncleanliness. He is breaking the Gentile barrier. In principle, therefore, there is no difference between the Jewish and Gentile sides of the lake. The cured man cannot join Jesus on his return trip to Galilee; he has to spread the news of the kingdom throughout the Decapolis (5:20). This also parallels the conclusion of the first exorcism on the Jewish side of the lake, when the man spreads word about Jesus throughout Galilee (1:28).

This story also alludes to two other familiar Markan themes, the ambiguity of miracles and the importance of a correct understanding of Jesus. The response of the crowd after Jesus has healed the demoniac is not faith but fear. As we have seen before, miracles by themselves do not necessarily lead to faith. They are open to several different interpretations. Mark's christological concerns are apparent at the end of this pericope when he parallels "Lord" and "Jesus." Jesus tells the man to, "Go home to your family and announce to them all that the *Lord* in his pity has done for you" (5:19). In the next verse Mark reports, "Then the man went off and began to proclaim in the Decapolis what *Jesus* had done for him; and all were amazed" (5:20). In spite of frequent clues concerning the identity of Jesus, for Mark a correct understanding of Jesus is only possible after his death and resurrection.

Jairus' Daughter; the Hemorrhaging Woman (5:21-43)

21 When Jesus had crossed again (in the boat) to the other side, a large crowd gathered around him, and he stayed close to the sea. 22 One of the synagogue officials, named Jairus, came forward. Seeing him he fell at his feet 23 and pleaded earnestly with him, saying, "My daughter is at the point of death. Please, come lay your hands on her that she may get well and live." 24 He went

off with him, and a large crowd followed him and pressed upon him. ²⁵ There was a woman afflicted with hemorrhages for twelve years. ²⁶ She had suffered greatly at the hands of many doctors and had spent all that she had. Yet she was not helped but only grew worse. ²⁷ She had heard about Jesus and came up behind him in the crowd and touched his cloak. ²⁸ She said, "If I but touch his clothes, I shall be cured." ²⁹ Immediately her flow of blood dried up. She felt in her body that she was healed of her affliction. ³⁰ Jesus, aware at once that power had gone out from him, turned around in the crowd and asked, "Who has touched my clothes?" ³¹ But his disciples said to him, "You see how the crowd is pressing upon you, and yet you ask, 'Who touched me?'" ³² And he looked around to see who had done it. ³³ The woman, realizing what had happened to her, approached in fear and trembling. She fell down before Jesus and told him the whole truth. ³⁴ He said to her, "Daughter, your faith has saved you. Go in peace and be cured of your affliction." ³⁵ While he was still speaking, people from the synagogue official's house arrived and said, "Your daughter has died; why trouble the teacher any longer?" ³⁶ Disregarding the message that was reported, Jesus said to the synagogue official, "Do not be afraid; just have faith." ³⁷ He did not allow anyone to accompany him inside except Peter, James, and John, the brother of James. ³⁸ When they arrived at the house of the synagogue official, he caught sight of a commotion, people weeping and wailing loudly. ³⁹ So he went in and said to them, "Why this commotion and weeping? The child is not dead but asleep." ⁴⁰ And they ridiculed him. Then he put them all out. He took along the child's father and mother and those who were with him and entered the room where the child was. ⁴¹ He took the child by the hand and said to her, "Talitha koum," which means, "Little girl, I say to you, arise!" ⁴² The girl, a child of twelve, arose immediately and walked around. (At that) they were utterly astounded. [43] He gave strict orders that no one should know this and said that she should be given something to eat.

After the exorcism of the Gerasene demoniac, Jesus returns to the Jewish side of the lake from which he and his disciples had set out in 4:35. When they arrive on the western side, Jesus performs two more healing miracles. He raises Jairus' daughter and cures the woman who has been hemorrhaging. Just as Mark has shown Jesus' lordship over nature (4:35-41) and demons (5:1-20), now he relates stories which highlight Jesus' lordship over sickness and death. These two cures give still more evidence of Jesus' power.

In these pericopes both Jairus and the woman get help because of their faith. They see Jesus as a vehicle of God's power. When the reader is told that Jairus' daughter seems to have died, the demand for faith becomes even greater. If we look more closely at the language Mark uses to tell these stories, we see a symbolic reference to Jesus' own resurrection and to Jesus as the bringer of salvation.

The use of the Greek verb *egeirein* (to arise) in 5:41 suggests that this story has symbolic significance for Mark and his readers. Elsewhere in Mark, and throughout the New Testament, this verb is generally used to express resurrection from the dead (cf. 6:14, 16) and Jesus' own resurrection (cf. 16:6). In a typical translation of 5:28, the woman says, "If I but touch his clothes, I shall be cured." The verb translated here as "cured" is also a technical term for "salvation." Therefore, verse 28 could just as easily be translated as, "If I but touch his clothes, I shall be saved." Verse 34 can similarly be translated as "Your faith has saved you."

Both these stories, therefore, contain hints about who Jesus is. As we have seen previously, however, one needs the eyes of faith in order to see this. Mark presents Jesus as the one who will be resurrected, the one who announces God's salvation, and the one who can exercise God's power over death itself. In spite of these hints, it would be easy for Jesus' initial audience to misunderstand this and to see him merely as a miracle worker, whose actions are unrelated to the inbreaking of God's kingdom. This is why Jesus issues the injunction to silence in the last verse of this pericope (5:41). A correct understanding of Jesus, according to Mark, must include the cross.

Mark's presentation of the kingdom of God as not exclusive is seen here, as it was in the call of Levi (2:13-14). The woman with the twelve-year hemorrhage would have been viewed as a perpetual menstruant and thus considered ceremonially unclean according to Old Testament purity laws (Lv 15:26-27). Touching things which she had touched meant polluting oneself; by touching other people, she made them unclean. Jesus does not avoid her, rather he blesses her, "Daughter, your faith has saved you. Go in peace and be cured of your affliction" (5:34). Jesus treated her as a person, in spite of her social and sexual stigma.

Jesus in His Hometown (6:1-6)

6:1 He departed from there and came to his native place, accompanied by his disciples. 2 When the sabbath came he began to teach in the synagogue, and many who heard him were astonished. They said, "Where did this man get all this? What kind of wisdom has been given him? What mighty deeds are wrought by his hands! 3 Is he not the carpenter, the son of Mary, and the brother of

James and Joses and Judas and Simon? And are not his sisters here with us?" And they took offense at him. [4] Jesus said to them, "A prophet is not without honor except in his native place and among his own kin and in his own house." [5] So he was not able to perform any mighty deed there, apart from curing a few sick people by laying his hands on them. [6] He was amazed at their lack of faith. He went around to the villages in the vicinity teaching.

Returning again to his hometown of Nazareth, Jesus teaches in the synagogue on the sabbath, amazing many with his wisdom. Jesus' identity is still foremost in Mark's mind as the Nazareth townspeople wonder about Jesus (6:2-3). Ultimately, however, this pericope concerns the rejection of Jesus by his own people. Thus, it continues the theme we saw first in chapter 3 above: Those who ought to have recognized his importance are the very ones who reject him. Just as his family and the religious authorities rejected him, so do relatives and neighbors in his home town. The Christian reader of Mark's Gospel, however, knows that God is the origin of Jesus' power. Jesus' rejection by the people of Nazareth, which ends this section of the Gospel, reminds many of the plot to destroy Jesus that ended the first part of Mark's Gospel (3:6).

Jesus Sends the Twelve (6:7-13)

The second half (6:7–8:21) of this large section of the Gospel (4:35–8:12) begins with Jesus instructing his disciples and preparing them for their part in his work. It will end on the theme of misunderstanding, as did the first part of this section, when Jesus says to his disciples, "Do you still not understand?" (8:21).

⁷ He summoned the Twelve and began to send them out two by two and gave them authority over unclean spirits. ⁸ He instructed them to take nothing for the journey but a walking stick—no food, no sack, no money in their belts. ⁹ They were, however, to wear sandals but not a second tunic. ¹⁰ He said to them, "Wherever you enter a house, stay there until you leave from there. ¹¹ Whatever place does not welcome you or listen to you, leave there and shake the dust off your feet in testimony against them." ¹² So they went off and preached repentance. ¹³ They drove out many demons, and they anointed with oil many who were sick and cured them.

Jesus calls the twelve and sends them out two by two to exercise the authority to preach and expel demons that he had given them as part of their initial call (3:13-19). Apparently Mark wants the reader to conclude that Jesus' rejection at Nazareth led him to take his message elsewhere and include the twelve more actively in his missionary enterprise. These missionaries left everything behind, as Jesus "instructed them to take nothing for the journey but a walking stick" (6:8)—no bread, no bag and no money. They are to avoid appearing like other missionaries in the Greco-Roman world, who make a good living out of their preaching. Their lack of possessions indicates that they believe God will sustain them on their missionary journey. Jesus also commands them to accept the hospitality of those who welcome them and to be content with it. They are not to move from one place to another looking for better conditions; they are to accept whatever is offered to them (6:10). Those who engage in this missionary enterprise without resources are dependent on the grace of God and the good will of the community to which they go. This calls for confidence, courage, and perseverance (they will not always be successful, cf. 6:11). They are being reminded to trust and to be dependent on God and not to seek security in themselves.

From this text, it is fair to conclude that genuine discipleship has a missionary dimension. It is not simply an interior spiritual quest. Those who were called to "be with" Jesus were also sent into the world to preach, exorcize and heal. Christian discipleship, therefore, is dynamic and not static.

For reflection: In the modern world the tension between being and doing is often brought into a conversation when someone inquires about the proper relationship between faith and social justice. What does faith mean for you? Is it a kind of knowing, a coming to awareness that leads to contemplation? Is faith a kind of illumination, which makes you see clearly what once was dark? Or is faith an assent to a determinate body of revealed doctrine? Is faith a firm assent to what the Church teaches in the name of God? Or is faith nothing other than personal trust in the love and goodness of God?

Regardless of how you answer these questions, can you call yourself a Christian if your understanding of faith excludes working for social justice? Must faith be more than interior assent? Must faith include obedience to God's will?

Death of John the Baptist (6:14-29)

14 King Herod heard about it, for his fame had become widespread, and people were saying, "John the Baptist has been raised from the dead; that is why mighty powers are at work in him." 15 Others were saying, "He is

Elijah"; still others, "He is a prophet like any of the prophets." [16] But when Herod learned of it, he said, "It is John whom I beheaded. He has been raised up." [17] Herod was the one who had John arrested and bound in prison on account of Herodias, the wife of his brother Philip, whom he had married. [18] John had said to Herod, "It is not lawful for you to have your brother's wife." [19] Herodias harbored a grudge against him and wanted to kill him but was unable to do so. [20] Herod feared John, knowing him to be a righteous and holy man, and kept him in custody. When he heard him speak he was very much perplexed, yet he liked to listen to him. [21] She had an opportunity one day when Herod, on his birthday, gave a banquet for his courtiers, his military officers, and the leading men of Galilee. [22] Herodias's own daughter came in and performed a dance that delighted Herod and his guests. The king said to the girl, "Ask of me whatever you wish and I will grant it to you." [23] He even swore (many things) to her, "I will grant you whatever you ask of me, even to half of my kingdom." [24] She went out and said to her mother, "What shall I ask for?" She replied, "The head of John the Baptist." [25] The girl hurried back to the king's presence and made her request, "I want you to give me at once on a platter the head of John the Baptist." [26] The king was deeply distressed, but because of his oaths and the guests he did not wish to break his word to her. [27] So he promptly dispatched an executioner with orders to bring back his head. He went off and beheaded him in the prison. [28] He brought in the head on a platter and gave it to the girl. The girl in turn gave it to her mother. [29] When his disciples heard about it, they came and took his body and laid it in a tomb.

Before he reports the return of the twelve, Mark narrates the story of Herod's beheading of John the Baptist. The "success story" of the mission of the twelve (6:7-13, 30) surrounds the story of John the Baptist's death. Once again we encounter Mark's use of intercalation (the sandwich technique). As stated earlier, when Mark uses this technique there is always a relationship between the "book ends" and what is in the middle. The obvious conclusion here is that discipleship might involve suffering and death; the fate of John the Baptist foreshadows that of Jesus and his disciples. This emphasis on the suffering and death of Jesus, and its importance for a correct understanding of Jesus and Christian discipleship, will become much clearer in the following chapters.

Return of the Disciples and Feeding of the Five Thousand (6:30-44)

30 The apostles gathered together with Jesus and reported all they had done and taught. 31 He said to them, "Come away by yourselves to a deserted place and rest a while." People were coming and going in great numbers, and they had no opportunity even to eat. 32 So they went off in the boat by themselves to a deserted place. 33 People saw them leaving and many came to know about it. They hastened there on foot from all the towns and arrived at the place before them. 34 When he disembarked and saw the vast crowd, his heart was moved with pity for them, for they were like sheep without a shepherd; and he began to teach them many things. 35 By now it was already late and his disciples approached him and said, "This is a deserted place and it is already very late. 36 Dismiss them so that they can go to the surrounding farms and villages and buy themselves something to eat." 37 He said to them in reply, "Give them some food yourselves." But they said to him, "Are we to buy two hundred days' wages worth of food and give it to them to eat?" 38 He asked them, "How many loaves do you have? Go and see." And

when they had found out they said, "Five loaves and two fish." [39] So he gave orders to have them sit down in groups on the green grass. [40] The people took their places in rows by hundreds and by fifties. [41] Then, taking the five loaves and the two fish and looking up to heaven, he said the blessing, broke the loaves, and gave them to (his) disciples to set before the people; he also divided the two fish among them all. [42] They all ate and were satisfied. [43] And they picked up twelve wicker baskets full of fragments and what was left of the fish. [44] Those who ate (of the loaves) were five thousand men.

After they return from their mission, the apostles go away with Jesus to rest. Many people hear about where they are going and follow them. Filled with compassion, Jesus teaches this multitude. It becomes late and the crowd has no food. Jesus takes what they have, five loaves of bread and two fishes, blesses it, breaks it, and distributes it. All five thousand eat until they are sated, and what is left over fills twelve baskets. The number twelve would have reminded Mark's readers of the fact that there were twelve tribes of Israel. This reinforces the fact that this feeding, which takes place on the western side of the lake, is directed to the Jews.

This miraculous feeding would probably have reminded the original audience of God feeding the Israelites in the desert (Ex 16) and of Elisha multiplying the barley loaves and grain in order to feed one hundred men (2 Kgs 4:42-44). The passage is obviously eucharistic, since at the Last Supper Jesus "took bread, said the blessing, broke it, and gave it to them" (Mk 14:22), the same sequence of actions reported in 6:41. This story also looks forward to and anticipates the eschatological banquet to be celebrated when God's kingdom comes in its fullness. After the words of institution (14:2-24), Jesus concludes the meal with the affirmation that this is the last cup of wine he will drink before his death. He looks forward to the day when he will "drink it anew in the kingdom of God" (14:25).

A close reading of Mark's first feeding story (6:32-44) reveals that Jesus does not take pity on the crowd because they are hungry, but because they are "like sheep without a shepherd" (6:34). Within the context of Mark's Gospel this points to a time after the death of Jesus. When he speaks to his disciples on the Mount of Olives after their final meal together (14:27), Jesus interprets Zechariah 13:7, "I will strike the shepherd, and the sheep will be dispersed," as referring to his own imminent death and the scattering of his disciples (14:50). This miracle addresses the absence of Jesus and the continuity of his reign.

The focus of the feeding of the five thousand is on the future, after the death of Jesus when the community will be leaderless. The disciples are commissioned to feed the people (make the crowds orderly and distribute bread). Jesus is showing them how to care for the people. They should be able, therefore, to assume their roles as shepherds when the need arises. Their desire to send the crowd away (6:35-36) and buy bread, suggests, however, misunderstanding. Jesus has established the kingdom on the Jewish side of the lake and, speaking about a time when his absence will be felt, has put the disciples in charge of continuing his mission.

For reflection: It is almost impossible for any group, even an apocalyptic sect living in expectation of an imminent final age, to survive without leadership and organization. The reader of Mark's Gospel, therefore, should not be sur-

NEW CITY PRESS
www.newcitypress.com
1-800-462-5980

Thank you for choosing this book.
If you would like to receive regular information
about New City Press titles, please fill in this card.

Title purchased: _____

Please check the subjects that are of particular interest to you:

- ☐ **FATHERS OF THE CHURCH**
- ☐ **CLASSICS IN SPIRITUALITY**
- ☐ **CONTEMPORARY SPIRITUALITY**
- ☐ **THEOLOGY**
- ☐ **SCRIPTURE AND COMMENTARIES**
- ☐ **FAMILY LIFE**
- ☐ **BIOGRAPHY / HISTORY**

Other subjects of interest: _____

(please print)

Name: _____

Address: _____

_____

_____

NEW CITY PRESS
202 CARDINAL RD.
HYDE PARK NY 12538

prised to find Jesus delegating special tasks to his initial followers. That some are singled out for leadership roles in the community should not be the focus of our attention. What is important is how leaders are chosen, what tasks they are given, and how leadership is to be exercised. How do you understand leadership in the Church?

Jesus at Prayer (6:45-46)

[45] Then he made his disciples get into the boat and precede him to the other side toward Bethsaida, while he dismissed the crowd. [46] And when he had taken leave of them, he went off to the mountain to pray.

Let us take a moment to look at Jesus' prayer life, to which Mark draws attention at least eight times (1:35; 6:41, 46; 7:34; 8:6f.; 14:22f., 32-39; 15:34). As early as the first chapter, after he has been healing and exorcizing demons and before he announces his preaching tour, we learn that Jesus rises early in the morning and goes out to a lonely place to pray (1:35). Here in chapter 6 he makes his disciples get in a boat and set sail for the other side of the Sea of Galilee, dismisses the crowd, and goes off on his own to pray (6:46).

Prayer is associated with mission in Mark, as Jesus prays before he embarks on his preaching ministry throughout Galilee (1:35) and before his second thrust into Gentile territory (6:46). In both feeding stories (6:41; 8:6, 7) and at the Last Supper (14:22, 23) Jesus delivers a table blessing or thanksgiving. Prayer is also used to praise God (cf. 2:12; 11:9-10) and for petition and intercession (cf. 11:24-25; 13:8; 14:32-39). It is clear that Jesus expects his followers to pray (cf. 11:24-25; 14:38).

Mark's presentation of Jesus at prayer suggests that Jesus' example is meant to be a model for his followers. Our author believes that prayer has an important role to play in the life of the Christian. Prayer is the way we communicate or dialogue with God. By means of prayer we offer our commitment to God and receive strength to do God's will.

For reflection: Is prayer a basic part of your life? Do you seek to communicate with God through prayer? In the Hebrew Bible much of the prayer of the people of Israel has to do with praise, thanksgiving, or intercession. How would you characterize your prayers? The early Christians used patterns of individual, communal and liturgical prayer they found in Jewish worship. Over the years greater emphasis came to be given to individual prayer, often referred to as meditation or contemplation. More recently, some Christians have begun to return to the ancient notion that liturgical prayer should be the center of the life of the Church and of individual piety. What is the place of liturgical prayer in your life? Is your personal prayer life centered on scripture? Should it be?

Jesus, Son of God (6:47-52)

[47] When it was evening, the boat was far out on the sea and he was alone on shore. [48] Then he saw that they were tossed about while rowing, for the wind was against them. About the fourth watch of the night, he came toward them walking on the sea. He meant to pass by them. [49] But when they saw him walking on the sea, they thought it was a ghost and cried out. [50] They had all seen him and were terrified. But at once he spoke with

them, "Take courage, it is I, do not be afraid!" [51] He got into the boat with them and the wind died down. They were (completely) astounded. [52] They had not understood the incident of the loaves. On the contrary, their hearts were hardened.

In their first voyage to the Gentile side of the lake (4:35-41), Jesus led the way and showed his disciples what to do. Now he makes the disciples lead the movement to Gentile territory (6:45). They fail to recognize Jesus, and even after he has been revealed they do not understand. They should have known that the feeding on the Jewish side of the lake was only a partial fulfillment of the kingdom. The first crossing should have opened their eyes to the inclusion of the Gentiles. The Markan Jesus reveals himself in the middle of the lake not merely as a miracle worker with powers over nature, but as the unifier who calmed the storm in order to secure passage to the Gentiles.

Focusing on the person of Jesus in this pericope, Mark suggests that he is even more than a unifier. The presentation of Jesus walking on water carries with it an implicit claim to divinity. In the Hebrew Bible it is Yahweh or Wisdom who is portrayed as walking on water (Ps 77:19; Jb 9:8; 38:16; Is 43:16; Sir 24:5-6). In the darkness of the fourth watch (between 3 A.M. and 6 A.M.), the disciples see Jesus walking on the sea, think he is a ghost, and panic. Jesus replies, as does Yahweh when he appears in Old Testament theophanies, "It is I, do not be afraid!" (6:50). It is likely that the "I am" or "It is I" alludes to the divine revelation formula found in the Hebrew Bible (Ex 3:14; Dt 32:39; Is 41:4; 43:10). The wind dies down, and the disciples are dumbfounded by what they have seen. If they had understood the symbolic feeding, they would not have been shocked to see Jesus walking on the water. Because they missed the symbols they were utterly astounded.

Mark suggests here that Jesus is no mere miracle worker but a divine being (i.e., the Son of God; cf. 1:1, 11; 9:7; 15:39). Mark implies that the disciples responded to this miracle in fear and confusion because they did not have a correct understanding of Jesus based on the feeding miracle. As we have said before, in Mark's view the disciples are unable to have this correct understanding prior to the cross.

Other Miracles (6:53-56)

[53] After making the crossing, they came to land at Gennesaret and tied up there. [54] As they were leaving the boat, people immediately recognized him. [55] They scurried about the surrounding country and began to bring in the sick on mats to wherever they heard he was. [56] Whatever villages or towns or countryside he entered, they laid the sick in the marketplaces and begged him that they might touch only the tassel on his cloak; and as many as touched it were healed.

With Jesus and his disciples now back on the eastern side of the lake, Jesus performs numerous healings. Thus the sequence found in chapter 1 on the Jewish side of the lake has now been repeated on the Gentile side: first exorcism and then healing.

Jesus and the Pharisees (7:1-23)

[1] Now when the Pharisees with some scribes who had come from Jerusalem gathered around him, [2] they

observed that some of his disciples ate their meals with unclean, that is, unwashed, hands. [3] (For the Pharisees and, in fact, all Jews, do not eat without carefully washing their hands, keeping the tradition of the elders. [4]And on coming from the marketplace they do not eat without purifying themselves. And there are many other things that they have traditionally observed, the purification of cups and jugs and kettles (and beds).) [5]So the Pharisees and scribes questioned him, "Why do your disciples not follow the tradition of the elders but instead eat a meal with unclean hands?" [6]He responded, "Well did Isaiah prophesy about you hypocrites, as it is written: 'This people honors me with their lips, but their hearts are far from me; [7] In vain do they worship me, teaching as doctrines human precepts.' [8]You disregard God's commandment but cling to human tradition." [9] He went on to say, "How well you have set aside the commandment of God in order to uphold your tradition! [10] For Moses said, 'Honor your father and your mother,' and 'Whoever curses father or mother shall die.' [11]Yet you say, 'If a person says to father or mother, "Any support you might have had from me is *qorban*"' (meaning, dedicated to God), [12] you allow him to do nothing more for his father or mother. [13]You nullify the word of God in favor of your tradition that you have handed on. And you do many such things." [14] He summoned the crowd again and said to them, "Hear me, all of you, and understand. [15]Nothing that enters one from outside can defile that person; but the things that come out from within are what defile." [[16]][17] When he got home away from the crowd his disciples questioned him about the parable. [18]He said to them, "Are even you likewise without understanding? Do you not realize that everything that goes into a person from outside cannot defile, [19] since it enters not the heart but the stomach and passes out into the latrine?" (Thus he declared all foods clean.) [20]"But what comes out of a person, that is what defiles. [21] From within people, from their hearts, come evil thoughts, unchastity, theft, murder, [22] adultery, greed, malice, deceit, licentiousness, envy, blasphemy, arrogance, folly. [23] All these evils come from within and they defile."

The admission of the Gentiles into the kingdom and into the Christian community was a sensitive issue. Here we read of opposition coming from Jerusalem and arguing that the Jewish food laws are binding on the Gentiles (7:2-3). Some Pharisees and scribes challenge Jesus for allowing his disciples to eat their meals with unwashed hands, a violation of the oral law formulated and handed down by the early Pharisees. Such rituals were very important to the Pharisees, because they maintained the wall of separation between the Israelites and the unclean Gentiles.

Old Testament law divided objects, persons, places, and animals into two categories, clean and unclean. Clean objects could be contaminated if they were merely touched by a contaminated person or animal. The Pharisees stressed eating with those who obeyed the purity laws (cf. 2:16) and washing one's hands before eating. This was necessary to cleanse them from any religious contamination, which they might have accidentally acquired during the day.

Jesus takes this conflict to another level with his counter question (7:6). He accuses his opponents of transgressing not a human convention but the commandment of God (7:6-13). The sin of the Pharisees arises out of a piety which ignores the teaching of the prophets. The hypocrisy here involves substituting legalisms for obedience to the true intention of the law. They have elevated merely human customs to the status of revealed doctrine.

The problem behind this pericope is that the Pharisees had encouraged people to dedicate their property to God as a gift. Once the property was promised to God (i.e., the temple) it could not be used to support one's parents. In practice, this meant that the giver could continue to use this piece of property, while denying its use to others. Eventually it would become the property of the temple. The result suggested here is that declaring something dedicated to God (apparently a very pious act) is actually a clever way to avoid one's responsibilities, one's religious obligations to one's parents. The Pharisees have encouraged this apparently pious act at the expense of human suffering.

Jesus then teaches about the traditional understanding of defilement and real defilement (7:14-23). Defilement basically means being unfit for fellowship with God and God's people. The question then is what makes a person unacceptable to God. The levitical tradition concluded that what one ate could cause such alienation. At issue here is whether the Gentiles have to conform to this Jewish practice or whether Jesus has liberalized the tradition in order to make room for the Gentiles. In his answer, Jesus tells his audience that the Jewish tradition is not just liberalized, it is no longer in force. Only moral evil can create such alienation from God. The focus should be on the internal (morality, the heart, one's conscience, one's motivation) and not on external ritual. Jesus condemned the oral tradition, which had taken on an idolatrous character and prevented obedience to God's will. He has given all people the freedom to eat together, both now and at the messianic banquet. The christological point is that Jesus is the authoritative interpreter of the Jewish law found in the Hebrew Bible.

Jesus sharply criticized the religious situation as he found it in contemporary Israel. He was periodically in controversy with Jewish men of power concerning the correct interpretation of the Jewish Scriptures and tradition. Unfortunately, the portrayal of Jewish hostility to Jesus and of the Jewish involvement in his condemnation and death have been used by some Christians down through the centuries to justify anti-Semitism. Jesus' suffering and death cannot be blamed on all the Jews then living, nor upon Jews living after the death of Jesus.

For reflection: All enduring human societies offer their members ways of making sense out of life by providing systems of meaning. These systems consist of largely imaginary lines drawn around self, others, nature, time, and space. When something is out of place according to the prevailing system it is considered wrong or deviant. In this pericope, Jesus asserts a clear rejection of the established Jewish purity system. What is it that the Christian community has put in its place? What is it that helps order your existence? Is Sunday morning a special time for you and your family, or is it just another day? Are you upset when children's baseball and soccer games are scheduled for Sunday morning? Should you be? Are there certain people with whom you would refuse to associate and whom you would not want your children to marry? Are you guilty of the sin of racism or classism? In examining your own invisible boundaries that help you to make sense out of life, you must ask yourself if you have confused a human construction with God's will. Has something become an absolute in your life that should really be seen as changeable? Have you confused a human composition with divine revelation?

Further Miracles among Gentiles (7:24-37)

> [24] From that place he went off to the district of Tyre. He entered a house and wanted no one to know about it, but he could not escape notice. [25] Soon a woman whose daughter had an unclean spirit heard about him. She came and fell at his feet. [26] The woman was a Greek, a Syrophoenician by birth, and she begged him to drive the demon out of her daughter. [27] He said to her, "Let the children be fed first. For it is not right to take the food of the children and throw it to the dogs." [28] She replied and said to him, "Lord, even the dogs under the table eat the children's scraps." [29] Then he said to her, "For saying this, you may go. The demon has gone out of your daughter." [30] When the woman went home, she found the child lying in bed and the demon gone.

The Markan Jesus now moves to the northernmost point of his ministry and exorcizes the daughter of a Gentile woman. Jesus has just declared null and void the laws about clean and unclean, which kept Jews and Gentiles apart. Now he acts in a manner consistent with his own teaching in one of his rare contacts with a Gentile. Jesus' comments to the woman imply that Gentiles cannot be the recipients of his powerful acts. Her response challenges this exclusivity and indicates that there is a place for Gentiles in God's plan of salvation. While Jesus' earthly ministry appears to have been restricted primarily to Israel, this story foreshadows the fact that the Church's mission after his death will include Gentiles. Her persistence is usually understood as faith, suggesting that

Gentiles who have faith in Jesus and his ability to help them are acceptable to God.

The controversy unit, which is embedded in this miracle, raises the issue of Jewish-Gentile priority. The answer, first the Jews and then the Gentiles, agrees with Mark's story thus far. Regardless of whether it has been exorcisms, healings or feedings, Jesus' activity from the first chapter on has always been first to the Jews and then to the Gentiles.

> [31] Again he left the district of Tyre and went by way of Sidon to the Sea of Galilee, into the district of the Decapolis. [32] And people brought to him a deaf man who had a speech impediment and begged him to lay his hand on him. [33] He took him off by himself away from the crowd. He put his finger into the man's ears and, spitting, touched his tongue; [34] then he looked up to heaven and groaned, and said to him, "Ephphatha!" (that is, "Be opened!") [35] And (immediately) the man's ears were opened, his speech impediment was removed, and he spoke plainly. [36] He ordered them not to tell anyone. But the more he ordered them not to, the more they proclaimed it. [37] They were exceedingly astonished and they said, "He has done all things well. He makes the deaf hear and (the) mute speak."

The healing of the Syrophoenician woman's daughter is followed by Jesus' healing of a deaf man. Jesus' command to the crowd that they not tell anyone about this (7:36) and the fact that they violate this directive focuses the reader's attention on the question of Jesus' identity. We are reminded that there is more to Jesus than the fact that he can heal the sick. The allusion to Isaiah 35:5-6 in the words of the crowd (7:37) suggests that Mark wants his readers to understand that Jesus is the agent of God's salvation and that Israel's glorious future is present in the ministry of Jesus.

Feeding of Four Thousand among the Gentiles (8:1-10)

8:1 In those days when there again was a great crowd without anything to eat, he summoned the disciples and said, 2 "My heart is moved with pity for the crowd, because they have been with me now for three days and have nothing to eat. 3 If I send them away hungry to their homes, they will collapse on the way, and some of them have come a great distance." 4 His disciples answered him, "Where can anyone get enough bread to satisfy them here in this deserted place?" 5 Still he asked them, "How many loaves do you have?" "Seven," they replied. 6 He ordered the crowd to sit down on the ground. Then, taking the seven loaves he gave thanks, broke them, and gave them to his disciples to distribute, and they distributed them to the crowd. 7 They also had a few fish. He said the blessing over them and ordered them distributed also. 8 They ate and were satisfied. They picked up the fragments left over—seven baskets. 9 There were about four thousand people. He dismissed them 10 and got into the boat with his disciples and came to the region of Dalmanutha.

Following the healing of the deaf man (7:31-37), we arrive at the second feeding story. The disciples of Jesus, who misunderstood the significance of the first lake crossing (4:35-41), have misunderstood the second as well, seeing it only as a dramatic nature miracle. The real significance of the trip across the sea has eluded them. They fail to see that Jesus is breaking down the barrier to the Gentiles. They fail to understand that both Jews and

Gentiles can become members of the kingdom of God and the new community of Jesus. The second time they all travel across the Sea of Galilee, Jesus makes his disciples go before him. He had shown them the way earlier; now it is up to them to conduct the mission to the Gentiles. This is suggested by the fact that Jesus feeds the four thousand because they have been with him for three days (8:2). Just as Jesus took pity on the Gentiles after three days, so his disciples will begin the mission to the Gentiles after the death and resurrection of Jesus.

Just as in the first feeding, here too we see Jesus' concern about the future. In the feeding of the five thousand he was looking forward to the time when they would be like sheep without a shepherd, and now he takes pity on them after three days. His disciples must remember that it was after three days that Jesus took pity on the Gentiles. The fact that the number seven appears in this pericope also indicates a Gentile connection. Numerologists are aware that seven implies completeness or fullness, and a group of Hellenists appointed to assist the twelve in Acts 6:1-6 are seven in number and are referred to as "the seven" (21:8). This suggests that the beginning of the Gentile mission is being projected into the time after the death and resurrection of Jesus. The disciples are again involved in the distribution and again miss the point.

The Pharisees (8:11-21)

[11] The Pharisees came forward and began to argue with him, seeking from him a sign from heaven to test him. [12] He sighed from the depth of his spirit and said, "Why does this generation seek a sign? Amen, I say to

you, no sign will be given to this generation." [13] Then he left them, got into the boat again, and went off to the other shore.

A kingdom open to the Gentiles is totally unacceptable to the Jews. The Pharisees demand a sign from heaven, a miracle on demand, to authenticate Jesus' mission. They insist that divine approval be demonstrated for what Jesus has done. Jesus refuses to give to this faithless group any sign. His miracles have been the sign; his mission is the message. No other sign is needed; none will be given. In the midst of all these signs and symbols the Pharisees neither see nor hear. After Jesus breaks the bread on the Jewish side of the lake, they criticize him about not washing his hands before eating. After the feeding on the Gentile side of the lake with its symbols, they come demanding a sign.

[14] They had forgotten to bring bread, and they had only one loaf with them in the boat. [15] He enjoined them, "Watch out, guard against the leaven of the Pharisees and the leaven of Herod." [16] They concluded among themselves that it was because they had no bread. [17] When he became aware of this he said to them, "Why do you conclude that it is because you have no bread? Do you not yet understand or comprehend? Are your hearts hardened? [18] Do you have eyes and not see, ears and not hear? And do you not remember, [19] when I broke the five loaves for the five thousand, how many wicker baskets full of fragments you picked up?" They answered him, "Twelve." [20] "When I broke the seven loaves for the four thousand, how many full baskets of fragments did you pick up?" They answered (him), "Seven." [21] He said to them, "Do you still not understand?"

After this encounter with the Pharisees, Jesus and his disciples set off again in the boat. This pericope, which ends this section of the Gospel and summarizes the meaning of what has gone before it, contains some of Jesus' harshest criticism of his disciples found in Mark's Gospel. Jesus chooses this time, at the end of his northern ministry, to castigate his followers for their lack of comprehension and to offer them some hints which, one assumes, should lead them to a proper understanding of his ministry thus far. The disciples seem to have missed the point of Jesus' words and deeds in the first half of the Gospel. They take things on a literal, worldly level, unable to realize the implications of Jesus' signs. The language Jesus uses to chastise them (8:17-18) is the same he used to talk about "those outside," who failed to understand the parables (cf. 4:11-12). Thus the disciples join those outside in their lack of understanding of Jesus. Jesus then reminds them of two things, the feeding of the five thousand and the feeding of the four thousand. The disciples are not much better than the Pharisees. They neither hear nor see the symbolic meaning of the number of full baskets of fragments they picked up after the two feedings.

The kingdom community has been established on both sides of the lake. The Gentiles are included in the reign of God on an equal basis with the Jews. A further symbol of this unity might be seen in the one loaf (8:14). Jesus, the Bread of Life according to John's Gospel, is with them in the boat as a sign of unity.

Conclusion

In 4:35–8:21 we see Jesus as the great unifier. No longer is there a gulf between Jewish and Gentile Christians. The kingdom of God is not split in two but unified. Mark uses traditional material at his disposal to tell the story. He transforms the miracles into signs. Jesus is still presented as a miracle worker of massive proportions, but he performs these miracles in the service of the kingdom and on behalf of its two-fold unity.

Mark's presentation of Jesus as a unifier is important for us today. Christians are reminded of this unity in the well-known passage in the Letter to the Ephesians, which speaks about one body, one Spirit, one hope, "one Lord, one faith, one baptism; one God and Father of all, who is over all and through all and in all" (Eph 4:4-6). Our task today is to balance unity and plurality, universality in the midst of particularity. What unites Christians is their basic attitude toward Jesus of Nazareth. In different times, in different places, and in different cultures, this belief has been expressed in different styles of worship, in different words and prayers and songs. What we must realize, as we enter the next millennium, is that Christianity is no longer a Western but a global religion. We must understand that our faith is at the same time local and universal.

Throughout his Gospel, Mark has pictured Jesus' behavior as a model to be emulated by his disciples. By presenting Jesus as a unifier, Mark is stating that there should be no racial or ethnic discrimination in the Christian community. This reminds many of Paul's famous saying, "There is neither Jew nor Greek, there is neither slave nor free person, there is not male and female; for you are all one in Christ Jesus" (Gal 3:28). Mark seems to agree with Paul. Both Jew and Gentile are able to be members of Jesus' new family and members of the kingdom of God. In addition to this stress on the unity of Jew and Gentile, Mark hints at sexual equality as well. In 4:35–8:21 there is a noticeable pattern of sexual parallelism. Jesus shows concern first for a man (the Gerasene demoniac), then for two women (Jairus' daughter and the hemorrhaging woman), for two more women (the Syrophoenician woman and her daughter), and finally for another man (the deaf mute). When one combines this with the fact that many women followed Jesus and obeyed his call to service (15:41), it appears that as far as Mark is concerned, there ought to be "not male and female" in the community of disciples. As members of the visible community we call the Church, all are called to become united as brothers, sisters, and mothers of one another and of Jesus.

IV
Service, Suffering and Discipleship
(8:22 – 10:52)

This central section appears to be the most carefully crafted one of Mark's entire Gospel. It is surrounded by two stories in which Jesus restores someone's sight: the blind man at Bethsaida (8:22-26) and blind Bartimaeus (10:46-52). These two pericopes represent the only times in this Gospel when Jesus gives sight to those who are physically blind. The compositional technique employed here, intercalation, is characteristic of Mark, as was mentioned earlier. Mark wants his readers to understand that what Jesus did at the beginning and the end of his journey (i.e., open the eyes of the blind), he also attempted to do while he was traveling along the way from Caesarea Philippi to Jerusalem. The miracle worker, who is able to cure physical blindness, sets out to cure the spiritual blindness of the disciples in between these two stories. In fact, throughout the central section of the Gospel, Jesus is pictured as opening the eyes of his disciples to a new dimension of his messiahship. These intimate companions of Jesus must "see" (i.e., understand) the necessity of his suffering and death, and what significance these have for a correct understanding of discipleship.

As Jesus moves from north to south, his identity, his purpose, and the requirements for discipleship should become clearer both to the disciples and to the readers of the Gospel. The disciples in Mark struggle with this new revelation about the suffering, death, and resurrection of Jesus. They have a difficult time understanding who Jesus is and what following him really requires. The reader of the first half of the Gospel, although in a better position than the Markan disciples, may have similar problems. What we must do now is travel with Jesus from Ceasarea Philippi to Jerusalem, examine the three discipleship discourses he delivers along the way, and allow our eyes to be opened to this new dimension of discipleship.

The Necessity of Jesus' Suffering (8:22-33)

22 When they arrived at Bethsaida, they brought to him a blind man and begged him to touch him. 23 He took the blind man by the hand and led him outside the village. Putting spittle on his eyes he laid his hands on him and asked, "Do you see anything?" 24 Looking up he replied, "I see people looking like trees and walking." 25 Then he laid hands on his eyes a second time and he saw clearly; his sight was restored and he could see everything distinctly. 26 Then he sent him home and said, "Do not even go into the village." 27 Now Jesus and his disciples set out for the villages of Caesarea Philippi. Along the way he asked his disciples, "Who do people say that I am?" 28 They said in reply, "John the Baptist, others Elijah, still others one of the prophets." 29 And he asked them, "But who do you say that I am?" Peter said to him in reply, "You are the Messiah." 30 Then he warned them not to tell anyone about him. 31 He began to teach them that the Son of Man must suffer greatly and be rejected by the elders, the chief priests, and the scribes, and be killed, and rise after three days. 32 He spoke this openly. Then Peter took him aside and began to rebuke him. 33 At this he turned around and, looking

at his disciples, rebuked Peter and said, "Get behind me, Satan. You are thinking not as God does, but as human beings do."

Thus far in the Gospel, Mark has presented Jesus as a miracle worker of massive proportions and as an authoritative teacher. But neither of these descriptions, nor both of them together, is a sufficient description of Jesus. Mark has alluded to the necessity of Jesus' suffering and death in earlier pericopes. However, it is in this section of the Gospel that this prominent Markan theme is really emphasized. What we find in these chapters is that three times Jesus predicts his passion, death, and resurrection, and each time he is misunderstood by his followers. Each of these misunderstandings is followed by a section in which Jesus teaches about what it means to be his follower.

Peter answers Jesus' question, "But who do you say that I am?" by stating "You are the Messiah" (8:29). Jesus immediately began to teach his disciples about the necessity of the suffering, death and resurrection of the Son of Man. This first passion prediction (8:31) is followed by Peter taking Jesus aside and rebuking him. Peter's confession is basically correct yet insufficient, because whatever the term "Messiah" meant to Peter it did not seem to include the idea of suffering. Because Jesus responds to Peter's rebuke by calling him "Satan," it is fair to conclude that anyone who denies the importance of the passion, death, and resurrection of Jesus stands on the side of Satan.

The disciples, who failed to grasp any of the earlier hints about Jesus' impending death, miss the point here as well. It would be difficult for Mark to say more clearly that Jesus' suffering was God's chosen way of redemption. Yet,

107

those who misunderstood the message of the two feeding stories and the message imbedded in the story of the death of John the Baptist, continue to misunderstand. Because they have an incorrect understanding of Jesus, they are unable to comprehend what he is telling them about the goal of his journey and the consequences of following him. They continue to think as human beings do, not as God does.

While there was no universally accepted description of the Messiah in first-century Judaism, the average person would probably have expected a triumphant Davidic ruler, who would lead the Jews in a successful attempt to overthrow the Roman government and inaugurate God's kingdom. If Peter can be credited with holding this position, then his puzzlement at Jesus' words about suffering and death is perfectly understandable.

For reflection: Examining ourselves, we must respond personally to Jesus' question, "Who do you say that I am?" As we do so, we cannot forget that Mark has presented Jesus as both the Son of God and as the suffering, dying, rising Son of Man. In your own christology have you stressed Jesus' divinity at the expense of his humanity? Have you been blind to the fact that Jesus of Nazareth was a human being in every sense except sin?

Since Mark presents Jesus as a model to be followed, we should examine what Jesus says and does and then pattern our lives on his. The task is made simpler in this section of the Gospel because Jesus responds to each misunderstanding of his passion-resurrection predictions by teaching his followers what discipleship entails.

Correct Understanding of "Discipleship" (8:34–9:1)

[34] He summoned the crowd with his disciples and said to them, "Whoever wishes to come after me must deny himself, take up his cross, and follow me. [35] For whoever wishes to save his life will lose it, but whoever loses his life for my sake and that of the gospel will save it. [36] What profit is there for one to gain the whole world and forfeit his life? [37] What could one give in exchange for his life? [38] Whoever is ashamed of me and of my words in this faithless and sinful generation, the Son of Man will be ashamed of when he comes in his Father's glory with the holy angels." [9:1] He also said to them, "Amen, I say to you, there are some standing here who will not taste death until they see that the kingdom of God has come in power."

The implications for discipleship of Jesus' modification of the title Messiah are found in 8:34-38. The context suggests that Jesus is talking about the possibility of martyrdom. He informs his disciples that they must not be ashamed of either him or his words. The logical conclusion is that if we adopt such a stance, then suffering and even death are possibilities. We must adopt a lifestyle in which faithfulness to Jesus and the gospel are more important than our own life. Nothing can be allowed to interfere with this total commitment to Jesus. This is a rather serious matter, since our eternal destiny depends on having the correct understanding of "Messiah," and on putting into practice the kind of discipleship which results from this understanding. Jesus promises final salvation to those who take up their cross and follow him (cf. 9:1). The ultimate goal of following Jesus, therefore, is to share in the glory of the coming Son of Man and the joys of the kingdom of God (9:1, 47; 10:15, 23-25).

As it stands in Mark's Gospel, this call to take up one's cross applies especially to those followers of Jesus who will be called upon to suffer martyrdom. The call to be faithful even if death results is a very difficult requirement. If death is seen as inevitable, one might muster up the courage to die with the dignity suggested in this passage. In most instances, however, believers who find themselves in dire straights are tempted by their persecutors with a choice: Renounce Jesus and his words and you will live; refuse to do so and you will die. The temptation is great, but the Markan Jesus urges us to remain faithful.

The problem here, of course, is that most Christians will never find themselves in such a life-or-death situation. If cross-bearing is taken too literally, then this particular demand of discipleship is irrelevant to the life of most disciples. Some readers have taken this text to mean that patient endurance is required in whatever trials, sorrows or disappointments one may meet. While this is a valid interpretation, we should be careful here not to dilute the message of Mark. After all, Jesus is talking about his own impending death on the cross, not the normal bumps and bruises of daily life.

In order to appreciate what is being said here, it is helpful to focus on the call to deny oneself. This should not be understood as denying things *to* the self, abstaining from certain luxuries. Jesus is speaking about the denial *of* the self, making ourselves not an end but a means. What is required, then, is to lead a non-egocentric existence. We should not be preoccupied with ourselves and the amassing of possessions (8:36), but with doing God's will. The follower of Jesus must be willing to make any sacrifice, even life itself, for Christ.

For reflection: The temptations most Christians face in their daily lives are usually quite subtle and insidious. In the workplace or in our dealings with others we are continually challenged in our attempt to conduct our lives according to the teachings of Jesus. Have you ever been involved in a business meeting where the conversation was driven exclusively by the "bottom line"? Have you been tempted to bring justice, human rights, and human dignity into the discussion, only to talk yourself out of it because it seemed inappropriate, thinking that it is better to save your job or livelihood than to lose it?

Some have adopted an attitude, consciously or unconsciously, which suggests that the teachings of Jesus should inform their private life (i.e., dealings with family and friends) but not their public life (i.e., business dealings). According to Mark's Gospel, can a Christian take this position?

At the very least, this passage invites us to reflect honestly on our past behavior. How many times have we been guilty of moral cowardice? We knew what we should have done, yet we chose to do something else, to take the easy way out. Most of the time, of course, we rationalize our behavior; usually we would not admit that we had been ashamed of Jesus and his words. Instead, we would talk about taking good care of our clients, the stockholders, or our families. We are capable of interpreting moral cowardice as heroic behavior. The question we need to ask ourselves, and to answer in total honesty, is whether what we have said or done suggests that we are ashamed of Jesus and his words. If we are, then Jesus tells us that the Son of Man will be ashamed of us when he comes in his Father's glory with the holy angels (8:38). If this is the situation in which we find ourselves today, we should take Jesus' advice, "Repent and believe in the gospel" (1:15).

Messiah, Son of Man, Son of God (9:2-34)

Mark invites the reader to ponder the identity of Jesus by the way he has arranged the story in this section of the Gospel. The spotlight is obviously on the person of Jesus when he asks, "Who do you say that I am?" (8:29). Peter immediately responds, "You are the Messiah" (8:29). Although Jesus does not actually reject this title, he never claims it for himself and does seem to have some reservations about it. He seems to prefer the title Son of Man. As Mark develops the story, however, it appears that ultimately Son of God is the preferred title for Jesus. In light of the previously mentioned general messianic expectation of the time (a political king and military leader), Jesus has corrected Peter's incomplete understanding by using the title Son of Man. But what is the meaning of this title?

In the Jewish Scriptures, Son of Man is used generically to mean human beings or humankind and to denote an apocalyptic, more than human, figure who will come "with the clouds of heaven" (cf. Mk 14:62) and be given power, glory and the kingdom (cf. Dn 7:13). In the Jewish book known as 1 Enoch (variously dated from 300 B.C.E. to 70 C.E.), the Son of Man appears as an eschatological judge and deliverer, who will overthrow the wicked and vindicate the righteous (1 Enoch 46-53).

Mark usually uses the title Son of Man in connection with one of his major themes, the humiliation, suffering, and death of Jesus. On occasion, however, he uses this term in apocalyptic sayings (cf. Mk 13:26; 14:62). It would seem, therefore, that Son of Man is one of Mark's preferred titles for Jesus. Both times Jesus is offered the title Messiah, he speaks about the Son of Man instead. And he is the only one to use this term in Mark. Neither his disciples nor his enemies refer to him as the Son of Man. It is a title that Mark seems to be using to correct the defective, erroneous, or ambiguous title Messiah.

This progression—from Messiah (8:29) to the Son of Man who must suffer, die, and rise (8:31)—culminates in the use of the most important christological title for Jesus in Mark when, at the Transfiguration, God intervenes to declare, "this is my beloved Son, listen to him" (9:7). Those who recognize Jesus as the Son of God must listen to what he says.

[2] After six days Jesus took Peter, James, and John and led them up a high mountain apart by themselves. And he was transfigured before them, [3] and his clothes became dazzling white, such as no fuller on earth could bleach them. [4] Then Elijah appeared to them along with Moses, and they were conversing with Jesus. [5] Then Peter said to Jesus in reply, "Rabbi, it is good that we are here! Let us make three tents: one for you, one for Moses, and one for Elijah." [6] He hardly knew what to say, they were so terrified. [7] Then a cloud came, casting a shadow over them; then from the cloud came a voice, "This is my beloved Son. Listen to him." [8] Suddenly, looking around, they no longer saw anyone but Jesus alone with them. [9] As they were coming down from the mountain, he charged them not to relate what they had seen to anyone, except when the Son of Man had risen from the dead. [10] So they kept the matter to themselves, questioning what rising from the dead meant. [11] Then they asked him, "Why do the scribes say that Elijah must come first?" [12] He told them, "Elijah will indeed

come first and restore all things, yet how is it written regarding the Son of Man that he must suffer greatly and be treated with contempt? [13] But I tell you that Elijah has come and they did to him whatever they pleased, as it is written of him."

Mark uses the Transfiguration scene to focus once again on the person of Jesus. Peter, James and John are granted a preview of Jesus as he will appear in his glorious state at the final coming of God's kingdom. Mark continues to look beyond suffering and death to Jesus' resurrection and parousia (the second coming of Christ at the end of history). It should be noted, however, that there is a balance achieved here between glory and suffering. As Jesus comes down the mountain following the Transfiguration (9:9-13), Peter, James and John engage him in a conversation concerning the Jewish belief that Elijah would come as a forerunner before the day of the Lord. In his answer there is a parallel drawn between Elijah and John the Baptist and between Yahweh and Jesus. Mention of the suffering of the Son of Man (9:12) and the fate of John the Baptist (9:13) remind the reader that passion and death precede resurrection and glory. Mark continues to demonstrate that he is interested in his readers having a correct christology.

[14] When they came to the disciples, they saw a large crowd around them and scribes arguing with them. [15] Immediately on seeing him, the whole crowd was utterly amazed. They ran up to him and greeted him. [16] He asked them, "What are you arguing about with them?" [17] Someone from the crowd answered him, "Teacher, I have brought to you my son possessed by a mute spirit. [18] Wherever it seizes him, it throws him

down; he foams at the mouth, grinds his teeth, and becomes rigid. I asked your disciples to drive it out, but they were unable to do so." [19] He said to them in reply, "O faithless generation, how long will I be with you? How long will I endure you? Bring him to me." [20] They brought the boy to him. And when he saw him, the spirit immediately threw the boy into convulsions. As he fell to the ground, he began to roll around and foam at the mouth. [21] Then he questioned his father, "How long has this been happening to him?" He replied, "Since childhood. [22] It has often thrown him into fire and into water to kill him. But if you can do anything, have compassion on us and help us." [23] Jesus said to him, "'If you can!' Everything is possible to one who has faith." [24] Then the boy's father cried out, "I do believe, help my unbelief!" [25] Jesus, on seeing a crowd rapidly gathering, rebuked the unclean spirit and said to it, "Mute and deaf spirit, I command you: come out of him and never enter him again!" [26] Shouting and throwing the boy into convulsions, it came out. He became like a corpse, which caused many to say, "He is dead!" [27] But Jesus took him by the hand, raised him, and he stood up. [28] When he entered the house, his disciples asked him in private, "Why could we not drive it out?" [29] He said to them, "This kind can only come out through prayer."

Several of the pericopes in the central section of Mark's Gospel draw our attention to issues we have examined before. The above story of the healing of the boy with a demon contains comments about the importance of faith and prayer. The pericope begins and ends with the focus on the disciples' inability to heal the boy. What is being highlighted, however, is the importance of faith, prayer, and the power of God operative in Jesus. Conscious reliance on God's power is needed when acting in Jesus' name.

For reflection: This pericope presents an interesting question for modern Christians. Do you believe that in some instances, when acting on Jesus' behalf, faith, prayer, and conscious reliance on God's power are necessary ingredients in order for you to be successful?

> [30] They left from there and began a journey through Galilee, but he did not wish anyone to know about it. [31] He was teaching his disciples and telling them, "The Son of Man is to be handed over to men and they will kill him, and three days after his death he will rise." [32] But they did not understand the saying, and they were afraid to question him. [33] They came to Capernaum and, once inside the house, he began to ask them, "What were you arguing about on the way?" [34] But they remained silent. They had been discussing among themselves on the way who was the greatest.

The response of Jesus' disciples after his second passion prediction (9:30-34) is similar to Peter's response (8:32) after the first passion prediction. Jesus and his disciples were traveling through Galilee when he began to teach them about the suffering, death, and resurrection of the Son of Man. But they did not understand (9:32). After the group settled into a house at Capernaum, Jesus asked them what they had been arguing about on the journey. Mark informs the reader that the disciples remained silent. While Jesus was speaking about his impending suffering and death, they had been discussing among themselves who was the greatest. They missed the implication that Jesus' greatness lies in the humility of his impending death. In spite of the fact that they have been following him for some time now, the disciples have an incorrect understanding of Jesus' identity and all that it entails.

Servants of All (9:35-41)

> [35] Then he sat down, called the Twelve, and said to them, "If anyone wishes to be first, he shall be the last of all and the servant of all." [36] Taking a child he placed it in their midst, and putting his arms around it he said to them, [37] "Whoever receives one child such as this in my name, receives me; and whoever receives me, receives not me but the one who sent me."

Following the second passion-resurrection prediction and the news that his disciples had been discussing which one was the greatest while Jesus spoke about his impending suffering and death, Jesus again comments on what discipleship entails (9:35). The word for servant used here is the term that would be used when referring to a waiter or waitress. It provides a stunning contrast to the talk of glory and privilege. Instead of a "we won, we're in charge" attitude, Jesus tips their idea upside down and tells his followers that they must be servants of all.

What does it mean to be a "servant of all"? Mark illustrates what he means when Jesus places a child in their midst (36-37). The focus in these verses is on the attitude of others toward the child. To "receive" a child in this context seems to mean to take care of or show kindness to. It suggests the kind of service that would be rendered to a guest.

A child in the Greco-Roman world was considered unimportant and had no status in the eyes of the world. But it is just such a person who must be the object of concern for the followers of Jesus. Serving all, including the powerless and helpless, is serving Jesus and his Father.

The radical nature of Jesus' teaching in these verses

becomes clearer when we realize that the verb translated here as "to serve" is often used to refer to male servants who wait on tables or to those performing so-called women's work. Whether this refers to waiting on tables, to daily housework or to the raising of children, it is seen as activity unbecoming for a free man to perform. One of the requirements for following Jesus, therefore, is to engage in a type of activity that by the secular society is considered acceptable only for women and servants.

Perhaps the type of service Jesus speaks of would be somewhat tolerable if performed for those who had wealth or status. It is conceivable that some benefits might accrue to the faithful servant of the rich and famous. But Jesus says that his followers must be servants of *all*, even those completely without status or power in the Greco-Roman world, such as children (9:37). Jesus teaches that true greatness means giving yourself in personal service to one from whom you can receive no benefit in return. Paradoxically, Mark informs his audience that it is in rendering such personal service to another that we meet Jesus and his Father (9:37).

A related theme appears in the following story about an exorcist who was driving out demons in Jesus' name, but was not considered one of his followers. Jesus warns his followers against intolerance adding that "whoever is not against us is for us" (9:40).

[38] John said to him, "Teacher, we saw someone driving out demons in your name, and we tried to prevent him because he does not follow us." [39] Jesus replied, "Do not prevent him. There is no one who performs a mighty deed in my name who can at the same time speak ill of me. [40] For whoever is not against us is for us.

⁴¹Anyone who gives you a cup of water to drink because you belong to Christ, amen, I say to you, will surely not lose his reward."

For reflection: Do you believe that only Christians can do God's will? Are you jealous when non-Christians seem to be more kind and compassionate to those in need? Do you have an "us versus them" attitude toward those outside the Christian community?

This passage instructs us to be tolerant of all those who are not actively opposed to Jesus and his teachings. Practically speaking, this has led Christians and non-Christians to work side by side on projects that are concerned with the universal common good. Those who recognize the dignity of the human person and the rights and obligations that flow from this conclusion are to be seen as allies and not as enemies. Do you conduct your life according to the principle that those who are not against you are for you?

On Temptation, Marriage, Children and Wealth (9:42–10:16)

The passages which occur next in the central section of this Gospel deal with issues of tempting others to sin (9:42-50), marriage, divorce, and children (10:1-16), and wealth and possessions (10:17-31).

⁴² "Whoever causes one of these little ones who believe (in me) to sin, it would be better for him if a great millstone were put around his neck and he were thrown into the sea. ⁴³If your hand causes you to sin, cut it off. It is better for you to enter into life maimed than with two hands to go into Gehenna, into the unquenchable fire. [44]45 And if your foot causes you to sin, cut it off. It is

better for you to enter into life crippled than with two feet to be thrown into Gehenna. [46]47 And if your eye causes you to sin, pluck it out. Better for you to enter into the kingdom of God with one eye than with two eyes to be thrown into Gehenna, 48 where 'their worm does not die, and the fire is not quenched.' 49 Everyone will be salted with fire. 50 Salt is good, but if salt becomes insipid, with what will you restore its flavor? Keep salt in yourselves and you will have peace with one another."

In 9:42-48 Jesus presents a harsh warning to those who would cause "one of these little ones" who believe in him to sin. A number of commentators believe that Mark intends for his readers to see these little ones as members of the community of Jesus' disciples. Jesus says it would be better for a person to be thrown into the sea with a millstone for a necklace than to scandalize one of these little ones. This harsh language is merely a strong metaphor and not meant to be taken literally. The point is that the salvation of the whole person at the end time is worth any sacrifice now.

For reflection: In the world of today this passage suggests that those in a position to influence others have a special responsibility to set a good example, or at least not to set a bad one. It seems obvious to most that religious leaders, politicians, teachers and parents fall under this charge. Others, however, suggest that those in leadership positions should not be held to such a high standard. The strong metaphor in this pericope indicates that sin is a very serious matter. Do you believe that personal sin is a serious matter? How do you react when you learn that someone in a position of authority has sinned in such a way that others have been led astray?

10:1 He set out from there and went into the district of Judea (and) across the Jordan. Again crowds gathered around him and, as was his custom, he again taught them. 2 The Pharisees approached and asked, "Is it lawful for a husband to divorce his wife?" They were testing him. 3 He said to them in reply, "What did Moses command you?" 4 They replied, "Moses permitted him to write a bill of divorce and dismiss her." 5 But Jesus told them, "Because of the hardness of your hearts he wrote you this commandment. 6 But from the beginning of creation, 'God made them male and female. 7 For this reason a man shall leave his father and mother (and be joined to his wife), 8 and the two shall become one flesh.' So they are no longer two but one flesh. 9 Therefore what God has joined together, no human being must separate." 10 In the house the disciples again questioned him about this. 11 He said to them, "Whoever divorces his wife and marries another commits adultery against her; 12 and if she divorces her husband and marries another, she commits adultery."

As Jesus begins his southern ministry (10:1), he is confronted by some Pharisees, who ask him a question about whether it is lawful for a man to divorce his wife (10:2). This is a peculiar question on the lips of a Pharisee, since Deuteronomy 24:1-4 clearly allows a husband to divorce his wife (although the wife could not divorce her husband). In first-century Judaism the dispute was not about the right to divorce but about what constituted valid reasons for divorce. The crucial text is Deuteronomy 24:1: "When a man, after marrying a woman and having relations with her, is later displeased with her because he finds in her something indecent" he may write her a bill of divorce, hand it to her, and send her out of his house. Some Jews concluded that this verse allowed for divorce only for the most serious causes (e.g., adultery), while others read this verse as permitting divorce for virtually any reason at all.

In its present context, Mark apparently sees the Pharisees as either testing Jesus' knowledge of the law or testing whether he will set himself against the law of Moses. Regardless of what Mark believes motivated the question, Jesus demonstrates in his answer that he is familiar with the Deuteronomy text, yet believes that two other texts from the Torah take precedence (Gn 1:27; 2:24). It is important to note that according to Mark what is prohibited is not divorce, but divorce and remarriage, or divorce in order to marry again.

Jesus interprets the Mosaic permission in Deuteronomy to divorce as a concession because of the hardness of human beings' hearts. They have demonstrated that they are simply unwilling to be taught and guided by the word of God. Ideally, there would be no divorce. Divorce is contrary to God's will in creating the human race. The husband and wife are joined together in the closest way possible, they become one flesh. God made human beings male and female so that they would enter into a lasting union.

The importance of this teaching is highlighted in verses 10-12 where the original saying of Jesus is extended to cover both sexes. Although verses 11-12 make the same point as verses 2-9, in effect they extend the teaching of Jesus beyond its original Jewish setting into the wider Greco-Roman world. A woman had the right to initiate a divorce (10:12) under Roman law, but not according to Jewish custom. These verses show that as the early Christian community encountered the Roman legal situation, it adapted this saying about marriage in order to preserve its original intention. According to Mark, Jesus teaches that marriage is willed by God, and that both husband and wife must understand the importance of maintaining the bond intact.

This would have been a difficult message for many to bear in the sexually permissive Roman society. The would-be Christian is being told that the cost of discipleship includes adopting a new sexual ethic, one which goes against the accepted values of the wider society. This teaching would have set Jesus and his followers apart from both the Jewish and pagan worlds in which they lived.

What can we conclude concerning marriage and divorce in the modern world based on this pericope? As we ponder this question there are several things that must be kept in mind. First, in order to come to any conclusion about the New Testament teaching on marriage and divorce, several other texts would have to be examined, including the famous "divorce exception clause" (Mt 5:32; 19:9; cf. 1 Cor 7:10-16). Second, if Mark 10:2-12 were read as legislation, this would seem to go against the trend of Jesus' teaching as a whole, which is against legalism. Third, although the Pharisees ask what is allowed (10:2, 4) Jesus responds in terms of what God has commanded (10:3, 7). These verses, therefore, can be said to present the ideal, to express God's will in this matter. The practical pastoral question concerning what is to be done if human sinfulness ("hardness of heart") persists, is not dealt with here. One must remember in interpreting this passage that in this pericope Jesus is not engaged in pastoral care but is setting forth what God requires. The permanence and sanctity of marriage is emphasized, and this is what the disciples are expected to uphold.

¹³ And people were bringing children to him that he might touch them, but the disciples rebuked them. ¹⁴ When Jesus saw this he became indignant and said to them, "Let the children come to me; do not prevent them, for the kingdom of God belongs to such as these. ¹⁵ Amen, I say to you, whoever does not accept the kingdom of God like a child will not enter it." ¹⁶ Then he embraced them and blessed them, placing his hands on them.

After a passage on marriage, a pericope dealing with children is perhaps appropriate. This story uses the child as an example of the kind of attitude needed by those who wish to enter the kingdom of God. The child is a very important symbol in this section of Mark's Gospel. The child symbolizes both the needy person the disciple of Jesus must serve (9:36-37) and the type of person the disciple must become (10:13-16). In the eyes of the ancient world a child was considered of little importance and had no social status. Since children were powerless and no one in society owed them anything, everything they received was the result of the love and generosity of their parents or other adults. In this Markan pericope, then, Jesus is telling his followers that one must receive the kingdom of God as a gift from God; they must realize that they are totally dependant on God. This demand for openness and acceptance is reminiscent of Jesus' first words in Mark's Gospel (1:14-15), where his call for faith includes the element of trust.

The Rich Young Man (10:17-31)

¹⁷ As he was setting out on a journey, a man ran up, knelt down before him, and asked him, "Good teacher, what must I do to inherit eternal life?" ¹⁸ Jesus answered

him, "Why do you call me good? No one is good but God alone. [19] You know the commandments: 'You shall not kill; you shall not commit adultery; you shall not steal; you shall not bear false witness; you shall not defraud; honor your father and your mother.'" [20] He replied and said to him, "Teacher, all of these I have observed from my youth." [21] Jesus, looking at him, loved him and said to him, "You are lacking in one thing. Go, sell what you have, and give to (the) poor and you will have treasure in heaven; then come, follow me." [22] At that statement his face fell, and he went away sad, for he had many possessions. [23] Jesus looked around and said to his disciples, "How hard it is for those who have wealth to enter the kingdom of God!" [24] The disciples were amazed at his words. So Jesus again said to them in reply, "Children, how hard it is to enter the kingdom of God! [25] It is easier for a camel to pass through (the) eye of (a) needle than for one who is rich to enter the kingdom of God." [26] They were exceedingly astonished and said among themselves, "Then who can be saved?" [27] Jesus looked at them and said, "For human beings it is impossible, but not for God. All things are possible for God." [28] Peter began to say to him, "We have given up everything and followed you." [29] Jesus said, "Amen, I say to you, there is no one who has given up house or brothers or sisters or mother or father or children or lands for my sake and for the sake of the gospel [30] who will not receive a hundred times more now in this present age: houses and brothers and sisters and mothers and children and lands, with persecutions, and eternal life in the age to come. [31] But many that are first will be last, and (the) last will be first."

As Jesus is traveling along, he issues an invitation to a rich man to establish an exclusive relationship with him (10:17-22). In order to follow Jesus, this individual would have had to leave behind all that he had. He would have had to part with what was dearest of all possible posses-sions in the ancient world, the family home and land. This is a rather tragic story. A person both desired to fulfill and actually fulfilled the commandments, yet he realized that more was necessary for salvation than merely following the rules. Jesus agreed with his conclusion and informed the man that he could attain his goal of eternal life only if he would sell what he had, give to the poor, and "follow me." But it was this that the rich man could not bring him-self to do.

One should resist the temptation to insist that this is an absolute requirement of Christian discipleship. In Mark's Gospel, Jesus consistently invites people to form a per-sonal relationship with him, not with a set of old or new rules and regulations. The command to sell all and give to the poor is not meant to be seen as just one more rule which everyone must follow. As far as we can tell, Jesus himself did not always require that everything be sold and the proceeds given to the poor (cf. 14:3-9). And although the literal following of the earthly Jesus seems to have been very important, Jesus did not always insist that his supporters leave everything in order to follow him (cf. 5:18-19).

The message of this pericope is that the appropriate response of every individual called by Jesus must involve absolute obedience and total devotion to God. Would-be followers of Jesus must rid themselves of anything and everything that prevents them from taking Jesus and his call seriously. The obstacle which stood in the way of the individual in this passage was his wealth. At this time, in this place, the vast possessions of this rich man prevented him from committing himself completely to Jesus.

Obviously, there are other things that could prevent a person from responding properly to Jesus. We must ask ourselves whether greed, anxiety about the future, or anything else is preventing us from committing ourselves totally to Jesus.

The fact that this command is specifically addressed only to this one individual, however, should not blind us to Jesus' overwhelmingly negative attitude toward riches. This approach may have been surprising to Jesus' original audience. In the early traditions of the Hebrew Bible, wealth is seen as a sign of divine favor. Riches do not present a problem, they are seen simply as a gift from God, usually with the understanding that there is a corresponding obligation to give alms to the poor. Jesus, therefore, has challenged the idea that riches are a sign of God's approval.

The position taken by Jesus is reminiscent of the attitude found in some of the prophets and in the Wisdom tradition. Wealth became a social and moral problem within Israelite society only when a social division arose between rich and poor. Amos, for example, says that the lifestyle of the rich results from their robbing the poor (Am 4:1; cf. 5:11; 8:4). The Book of Proverbs warns that poverty and wealth are dangerous because they can lead people to be forgetful of God (Prv 29:13; 30:7-9). According to the Book of Sirach, wealth is not wrong, but it is difficult for the rich to remain honest and faithful to God (Sir 31:1-11).

The addition of verses 23-25 to this pericope has the effect of changing the focus from one individual, his possessions and Christian discipleship, to rich people in general, their possessions and entry into the kingdom of God.

The question is can the rich be saved. Jesus does not say explicitly that it is impossible for the rich to enter the kingdom of God, but his hyperbolic comparison of a camel (Palestine's largest animal) passing through a needle's eye (smallest of commonly known openings) implies that it is virtually impossible. A person's wealth can easily stand in the way of total obedience to God; it can give the individual a false sense of security and independence. Riches can also lead to the oppression and exploitation of the poor and defenseless. Jesus probably issues these warnings about the dangers of wealth and vast possessions because in Palestinian society riches had already become a widely recognized source of alienation from God and oppression of the poor. Rich people were considered thieves or heirs of thieves; to be rich was, by definition, to be greedy.

Jesus points out that the salvation of the rich is possible, but only through the power of God (10:27). The point of this saying is that God will have to work the miracle of conversion in the hearts of the rich in order for them to be saved. It is so hard for those who have wealth to divest themselves of their material possessions, and the power and security that seem to come with them, that it will take divine intervention to free the rich from their bondage. If they are to enter the kingdom of God, rich people must take the steps necessary to cease being egocentric and to begin living for others. They must be freed from their enslavement to material goods and possessions. They must be free to use their riches properly, in the service of all.

For reflection: While many things can stand in the way of one's relationship with God, our modern absorption with wealth and possessions in the so-called first world suggests that the example used in this pericope continues to be relevant today. Many of us suffer from the afflictions of spiritual lukewarmness and political and economic conformity. A lack of faith and a failure to understand what conversion means leads to preoccupation with money, power and success. Are self-discipline and self-sacrifice values in your life? Do you understand the difference between "wants" and "needs"? Despite your material success, do you continue to say to others that you are "just getting by"?

Throughout the New Testament, wealth is seen as a great spiritual danger and, most often, as an absolute hindrance to trust in God. The rich are continually held responsible for the sufferings of the poor, while God is portrayed as the deliverer of the oppressed. God has chosen the side of the poor. Sharing with the poor is not regarded as an option, but as the normal consequence of faith in God.

In Mark 10:17-31, the focus soon shifts from the rich man who was unable to commit himself completely to Jesus because of his possessions to the difficulties any disciple might face in seeking to enter the kingdom of God. The "many possessions" (10:22) of the rich man have become house, brothers, sisters, mother, father, children, and lands (10:29). No longer is the discussion about almsgiving; now the focus is on the requirement for radical renunciation and separation from all that stands in the way of total commitment to the person of Jesus.

The promise of Jesus is that those who sacrifice in this manner will receive a great reward in the present and in the future. Those who follow Jesus, who leave everything behind in order to do God's will, are promised by Jesus that they will have, "now in this present age: houses and brothers and sisters and mothers and children and lands, with persecutions, and eternal life in the age to come" (10:30-31). The first part of this list points to the new relationships the disciple will have within the Christian community as a result of conversion. By mentioning persecutions, Mark has once again drawn our attention to the importance of the suffering of Jesus and of those who choose to go after him. One must follow Jesus for the right reasons, therefore, and not because one expects life will be more enjoyable and filled only with pleasant rewards.

Because the rich man was unable to separate himself from his many possessions, the group that followed Jesus was one fewer than it might have been. In spite of the fact that the rewards of discipleship far surpass the sacrifices, both now and in the future, this individual was unable to make the correct decision. The point being made here should not escape us: Jesus' call to discipleship can be refused. There is a choice involved.

Slaves of All (10:32-45)

The three-fold pattern, mentioned earlier, of passion-resurrection prediction followed by misunderstanding followed by Jesus' teaching about the correct understanding of discipleship is found again in the verses that occur next.

> ³² They were on the way, going up to Jerusalem, and Jesus went ahead of them. They were amazed, and those who followed were afraid. Taking the Twelve aside

130

again, he began to tell them what was going to happen to him. [33] "Behold, we are going up to Jerusalem, and the Son of Man will be handed over to the chief priests and the scribes, and they will condemn him to death and hand him over to the Gentiles [34]who will mock him, spit upon him, scourge him, and put him to death, but after three days he will rise." [35]Then James and John, the sons of Zebedee, came to him and said to him, "Teacher, we want you to do for us whatever we ask of you." [36] He replied, "What do you wish (me) to do for you?" [37]They answered him, "Grant that in your glory we may sit one at your right and the other at your left." [38]Jesus said to them, "You do not know what you are asking. Can you drink the cup that I drink or be baptized with the baptism with which I am baptized?" [39] They said to him, "We can." Jesus said to them, "The cup that I drink, you will drink, and with the baptism with which I am baptized, you will be baptized; [40]but to sit at my right or at my left is not mine to give but is for those for whom it has been prepared." [41] When the ten heard this, they became indignant at James and John.

The third prediction of the suffering, death, and resurrection of the Son of Man takes place as Jesus and his disciples are going up to Jerusalem (10:32). Because of Mark's narrative comments, it is impossible to miss the point that Jesus is speaking about himself and what will happen to him soon. The disciples of Jesus do manage to misunderstand once again, as is evident from the sons of Zebedee approaching Jesus and asking him to sit at his left and right in his kingdom. They apparently do not realize that Jesus' glory cannot occur before he dies.

[42]Jesus summoned them and said to them, "You know that those who are recognized as rulers over the Gentiles lord it over them, and their great ones make their

authority over them felt. [43] But it shall not be so among you. Rather, whoever wishes to be great among you will be your servant; [44] whoever wishes to be first among you will be the slave of all. [45] For the Son of Man did not come to be served but to serve and to give his life as a ransom for many."

Jesus' words after the third passion-resurrection prediction and the misunderstanding of James and John are reminiscent of the second discipleship discourse (9:35-37) in that the misunderstanding of the disciples is concerned with greatness or power, and Jesus contrasts the way of power and the way of service in his response (10:43). Jesus uses even stronger language here than he did in the discipleship discourse following the second passion-resurrection prediction. Here he informs his disciples that whoever would be first must be "the slave of all" (10:44).

Slaves were despised and rejected by both Jews and Greeks in the first century. They were considered to be property, on a lower level of humanity than those who were free. Thus, this teaching of Jesus represents an especially dramatic reversal of worldly standards. The type of service Jesus requires of his followers is precisely that which was scorned and rejected by the world in which he lived. The reason for the reversal of statuses is set out in 10:45. It is based on the behavior of the Son of Man, who served others and gave his life as a ransom to set others free. Jesus did not come to be served, but to serve.

These last two passages on discipleship talk about adopting a lifestyle that is service-oriented, because that is how Jesus led his life. Jesus' comments after the first passion-resurrection prediction indicate that conducting one's life in this manner might result in having to suffer

for the faith. Often it is the suffering of Jesus, and by implication that of his followers, that garners the attention of
the reader rather than the service theme. The idea that
Christian discipleship involves suffering is widespread in
the New Testament. A problem arises, however, when
individuals come to the conclusion that the best Christian
is the one who suffers the most for the faith. This has led
perfectly healthy people to do some rather strange things
to inflict pain on themselves. A correct understanding of
this section of Mark's Gospel sees that the focus of discipleship is on service, not suffering.

For reflection: Jesus came to serve, not to be served, and to
give his life for others. In conducting his life according to
God's will, he suffered, died, and was raised to everlasting
life. Are you prepared to see him as a model to be followed
and to live your life in the service of others? Will you be
surprised if as a result you experience discrimination, persecution and suffering? Will you accept this suffering with
the faith and hope that Jesus' ultimate fate, a life of glory
with God, will be your own? Discipleship means being prepared for service and suffering. Until the Son of Man
comes in glory (8:38) the Church's path will be difficult
though full of promise, for that is the way that Jesus
walked while on earth.

Church Leadership

This idea of service is extended to the type of leadership
that ought to characterize the Christian community. Jesus
says, "You know that those who are recognized as rulers
over the Gentiles lord it over them, and their great ones

make their authority over them felt. But it shall not be so among you" (10:42-43). The world labels as great those who dominate others, those who use their political or economic power to force the powerless to do their will. Frequently this kind of power leads to an abuse of the weak and defenseless so that the powerful might achieve their own ends. This worldly greatness is not to be the way of the disciples of Jesus. Followers of Jesus are to reverse this customary practice whereby those in authority rule by force. Mark could have had in mind here the typical Roman family in which the father had life and death power over his wife, children, servants, and slaves. Jesus specifically states that it should not be that way in the Christian community; service should be the goal behind relationships among the followers of Jesus. Mutuality and not dominance is what is required.

Mark has earlier described the community of Jesus' disciples as a family (3:34-35). As far as we can tell, social relations in the community of the disciples of Jesus mirrored the pattern of relations in the ancient family. Ideally all members of this new family were to be treated with due honor, support, and protection as members of the same household. Although fellowship characterizes Christian social relations, we should not imagine an absolutely egalitarian or communistic group. The same social structures and classifications found in the natural family in first-century Palestine characterize the Christian community as well; family structure at this time in history was not egalitarian. It is interesting to note, however, that while "father" is included in what one might have to give up (10:29), it is omitted from the list of relatives one will gain from following Jesus (10:30). The absence of a new father

134

might be because the disciple has only one father, God. But it is also possible that the term father is too symbolic of patriarchal domination, and Mark's view of the Christian community is much more egalitarian.

Behind the comments of Jesus here is the abuse of power common in the ancient (and modern?) world. For this model of leadership Jesus substitutes the ancient family ideal that individuals should always seek the good of the group and not pursue individualistic objectives. This allows us to talk about diverse and mutually dependent functions in the community. The motivating force behind relationships within the community of disciples should be selfless love and mutual care. Jesus' style of service brought neither personal financial gain nor social prestige. In fact, his service was rewarded by outrage from the authorities and a violent death. Jesus' model of service did not involve catering to the well-to-do, who might be able to reward him handsomely for his service. Rather, he directed his service to the outcasts of society, those with no political or economic power, the marginalized. These people, the most vulnerable in society, are the ones who need the Christian community the most.

For reflection: Do you follow Jesus' example by speaking out for those with no one to speak for them, defending the defenseless, seeing things as the poor and powerless do, and assessing all realities from their impact on the poor?

Is your experience of leadership in the Church consistent with Mark's description of servant discipleship? Many find themselves, by virtue of office, position, or relationship, having the right to command obedience from others. The authority one has to issue a command usually is enhanced by the external power that can be brought to bear to ensure that the command is carried out. If you presently occupy a leadership position in your faith community, how would you characterize your leadership style? Do you attempt to exercise your authority for the good of the group, as a servant of all?

Conclusion (10:46-52)

> [46]They came to Jericho. And as he was leaving Jericho with his disciples and a sizable crowd, Bartimaeus, a blind man, the son of Timaeus, sat by the roadside begging. [47] On hearing that it was Jesus of Nazareth, he began to cry out and say, "Jesus, son of David, have pity on me." [48] And many rebuked him, telling him to be silent. But he kept calling out all the more, "Son of David, have pity on me." [49]Jesus stopped and said, "Call him." So they called the blind man, saying to him, "Take courage; get up, he is calling you." [50] He threw aside his cloak, sprang up, and came to Jesus. [51] Jesus said to him in reply, "What do you want me to do for you?" The blind man replied to him, "Master, I want to see." [52] Jesus told him, "Go your way; your faith has saved you." Immediately he received his sight and followed him on the way.

When Jesus opens the eyes of Bartimaeus, at the end of this section of the Gospel, he and his disciples are leaving Jericho. Only fifteen miles from Jerusalem, the long journey they began at Caesarea Philippi is now almost finished. Three times along the way from north to south Jesus has tried to open the eyes of the spiritually blind disciples. And three times these disciples have failed to understand that it was necessary for the Messiah to suffer and die. In the end, their eyes have not been opened to this new dimension of messiahship. Their focus is on future glory, not on servant discipleship.

In the second and third discipleship discourses, Jesus informs his followers of the need to be servants of all (9:35) or slaves of all (10:44). In the Greco-Roman world of Jesus, serving the poor and serving children would have been distasteful. In the ancient world, children had little status within the community or family. A minor child was on a par with a slave, and was determined to be a free person who could inherit the family estate only upon reaching maturity. But Jesus makes no racial, social, or sexual distinctions when he tells his disciples that it is everyone ("all") whom they must serve. Jesus himself provides us with a model of this radical service when he dies on the cross so that others might be free. Would-be disciples must follow the way of Jesus, the way of the one who has come not to be served, but to serve. Can your following of Jesus be described as servant discipleship?

V

Jesus and his Disciples in Jerusalem
(11:1 – 13:37)

Jesus and his followers now arrive at their destination, Jerusalem, where Jesus' predictions of his suffering, death, and resurrection will be fulfilled. Mark describes Jesus' activity in this section of the Gospel as taking place on three consecutive days (11:1, 12, 20). On the first day we find the entry into Jerusalem. On the second, the cleansing of the temple. The third day features a series of stories that are set in and around the temple. Jesus then leaves the temple area, ascends the Mount of Olives, and delivers an apocalyptic discourse.

Jesus' Entry into Jerusalem (11:1-11)

^{11:1} When they drew near to Jerusalem, to Bethphage and Bethany at the Mount of Olives, he sent two of his disciples ² and said to them, "Go into the village opposite you, and immediately on entering it, you will find a colt tethered on which no one has ever sat. Untie it and bring it here. ³ If anyone should say to you, 'Why are you doing this?' reply, 'The Master has need of it and will send it back here at once.'" ⁴ So they went off and found a colt tethered at a gate outside on the street, and they untied it. ⁵ Some of the bystanders said to them, "What are you doing, untying the colt?" ⁶ They answered them just as Jesus had told them to, and they

permitted them to do it. [7] So they brought the colt to Jesus and put their cloaks over it. And he sat on it. [8] Many people spread their cloaks on the road, and others spread leafy branches that they had cut from the fields. [9] Those preceding him as well as those following kept crying out: "Hosanna! Blessed is he who comes in the name of the Lord! [10] Blessed is the kingdom of our father David that is to come! Hosanna in the highest!" [11] He entered Jerusalem and went into the temple area. He looked around at everything and, since it was already late, went out to Bethany with the Twelve.

The first pericope in this section of the Gospel depicts Jesus moving from Bethany to Jerusalem and its temple and back to Bethany. One must be careful not to read this episode in Mark through the eyes of the other evangelists. Based on Palm Sunday celebrations (both the palms and Sunday come from John's account) in which they have participated, many modern readers envision crowds of people from Jerusalem coming out to join the procession. They picture Jesus entering Jerusalem, and going up to and cleansing the temple. This simply is not the case in Mark's Gospel. There is no indication that people from Jerusalem came out to participate in the procession; it appears that the group taking part was limited to the followers of Jesus. The mention of "leafy branches that they had cut from the fields" (11:8) suggests a rural setting for this story. According to Mark 11:11 (not included by either Matthew or Luke), Jesus withdrew from the city on this day and returned to cleanse the temple on the following day.

As Mark tells the story, Jesus entered Jerusalem unobserved and un-applauded. The acclamation scene takes place out of reach of Jerusalem. It should not be missed, however, that Jesus enters Jerusalem as the prophet of the coming messianic kingdom. In Jewish apocalyptic writing, the cataclysmic battle of the last day was sometimes depicted as taking place on the Mount of Olives (cf. Zec 14:4). Because this is the location from which Jesus enters Jerusalem, Mark is often seen as suggesting that the eschatological events are taking place. In riding into Jerusalem on an ass, Jesus fulfills the prophecy of Zechariah 9:9, according to which the Lord as a divine warrior will ride into Jerusalem seated on the foal of an ass. The act of riding on the colt is thus a symbolic prophetic gesture. In times of war the king rode on a horse (Ex 14:9; Zec 17-11); the ass is instead the symbol of peace (Gn 49:11; 1 Kgs 1:33). Mark is presenting Jesus as the true messianic prophet-king for whom Jerusalem has been hoping for years. The Messiah has come to the holy city of Jerusalem.

His followers greet Jesus with words from Psalm 118:25-26. In most English versions of this text the cry of these disciples, the Aramaic Hosanna, is not translated, because it appears in Aramaic in the Greek New Testament. The word means "Help us!" or "Save us!" or "Rescue us!"

For reflection: Have you ever found yourself in a life-threatening situation? Did you see Jesus as one who could rescue you from that predicament? Is it accurate to describe ourselves and our planet as involved in a life-threatening situation and in need of salvation? Do you have faith that Jesus is able to rescue us from this dangerous predicament?

The Temple (11:12-25)

[12] The next day as they were leaving Bethany he was hungry. [13] Seeing from a distance a fig tree in leaf, he went over to see if he could find anything on it. When he reached it he found nothing but leaves; it was not the time for figs. [14] And he said to it in reply, "May no one ever eat of your fruit again!" And his disciples heard it. [15] They came to Jerusalem, and on entering the temple area he began to drive out those selling and buying there. He overturned the tables of the money changers and the seats of those who were selling doves. [16] He did not permit anyone to carry anything through the temple area. [17] Then he taught them saying, "Is it not written: 'My house shall be called a house of prayer for all peoples'? But you have made it a den of thieves." [18] The chief priests and the scribes came to hear of it and were seeking a way to put him to death, yet they feared him because the whole crowd was astonished at his teaching. [19] When evening came, they went out of the city. [20] Early in the morning, as they were walking along, they saw the fig tree withered to its roots. [21] Peter remembered and said to him, "Rabbi, look! The fig tree that you cursed has withered." [22] Jesus said to them in reply, "Have faith in God. [23] Amen, I say to you, whoever says to this mountain, 'Be lifted up and thrown into the sea,' and does not doubt in his heart but believes that what he says will happen, it shall be done for him. [24] Therefore I tell you, all that you ask for in prayer, believe that you will receive it and it shall be yours. [25] When you stand to pray, forgive anyone against whom you have a grievance, so that your heavenly Father may in turn forgive you your transgressions."

Mark describes the day following Jesus' initial entry into Jerusalem and the day after that in the above section using his familiar intercalation (sandwich) technique. The cursing of the fig tree and its outcome surrounds the story of the commotion in the temple and its outcome. The fig tree represents the temple, the center of Jewish cultic practices. What has happened to the tree foreshadows what will happen to the temple. Mark uses the fig tree to interpret the significance of Jesus' prophetic symbolism in the temple. Ultimately, the temple itself will be destroyed.

Why will the temple be destroyed? Many readers mistakenly conclude that Jesus is upset because the sellers are engaged in dishonest business practices or that this is the wrong location to conduct such business. Jesus is demonstrating instead that the practices necessary for the normal functioning of the temple must come to an end. His is a direct attack on the priestly leadership, a prophetic protest against what the temple has become.

Buying and selling were conducted in the outermost court, the court of the Gentiles. Here the money changers exchanged various Greek and Roman coins for pure money, Jewish or Tyrian coins, to be used for temple offerings. Sheep and goats for sacrifice were sold to pilgrims who had come from a distance; doves were used primarily by the poor (Lev 12:6-8; 14:22).

If the sacrificial animals cannot be purchased, there can be no sacrifice. If the money proper for paying the half shekel temple tax cannot be obtained, then monetary support of the temple and its priesthood would end. If no vessels can be moved within the temple, then cultic activity must cease. Mark presents Jesus as the prophet who strikes at the center of the Jewish religion; he shuts the temple down. The chief priests and scribes understand the symbolism involved in Jesus' act. The plot against Jesus' death intensifies (Mk 11:18), rising to a level we have not seen since the second sabbath violation back in Galilee (cf. 3:6).

Jesus said, "Is it not written: 'My house shall be called a house of prayer for all people'? But you have made it a den of thieves" (11:17). This citation is from the temple sermon of Jeremiah (Jer 7:11). In its setting in Jeremiah, calling the temple a den of robbers does not refer to dishonest practices within the temple walls. The robbers' cave is the place of retreat *after* the robbers have committed their crimes. People think that as long as temple services are continued they may retreat there, no matter how they have acted outside. They think that they can still find fellowship and forgiveness even if they have no intention of changing their behavior. Jesus' words are directed against the idea that no matter what people do, they are safe from punishment in the temple (cf. Jer 7:9-15).

The temple of God has been abused in two ways. Many were using it in a formal, mechanical manner. The implication is that there is little or no connection between external religious practices like worshiping at the temple and one's daily life in the workplace or at home. Like the people at the time of Jeremiah, Jesus, and Mark, individuals today often see their lives divided into religious and secular activities. The citation from Jeremiah also suggests that the temple was intended as a house of prayer for all nations. Mark's theme of inclusivity is again brought to mind. As we have seen before, he sees the inclusion of the Gentiles in salvation as an important part of God's plan which Jesus announces. Therefore, God has no further need for the temple. The good news will be proclaimed to the Gentiles only after Jesus' death; now is not the right time for the final consummation in the temple. The locus for finding God has shifted from the temple to Jesus.

This understanding serves to explain why seemingly

inappropriate sayings about faith and prayer actually have a place in this pericope (11:22-25). Faith and prayer, not the temple cult, are the way to God. One finds God through Jesus, faithful prayer, and enacting God's loving forgiveness of us in our treatment of our fellow human beings.

For reflection: This passage causes us to reflect on several things. Do we see our lives as an integrated whole, or as two separate parts? Do we operate with one set of values in our dealings with friends, family, and our religious community, and with a different set in our dealings with those outside these groups? Is it important to treat our neighbors justly, or is it enough to attend worship services each week? Is it permissible to oppress the immigrant, to take advantage of the weaker members of the community, to steal, murder, commit adultery, perjury, and idolatry, as long as we spend an hour or so in church on the weekend? In other words, is the "robbers' den" mentality alive and well in some people's attitudes today toward Church-related activities?

These comments about the temple cause us to reflect on our attitude toward the Church. When you hear the word "church," do you think first of a building? Or do you think of a community of God's people, called together by the Spirit in order to follow the teachings and lifestyle of Jesus and to worship publicly in his memory? Why do you gather together with your faith community on the weekend? Is it because someone told you that this hour was important? Or do you come together with faith in God, in recognition of the communal dimension of Christianity, the desire for communal prayer, a need for help in order to lead your life according to Jesus' teachings?

144

Origins of Jesus' Authority (11:27-33)

[26]27 They returned once more to Jerusalem. As he was walking in the temple area, the chief priests, the scribes, and the elders approached him 28 and said to him, "By what authority are you doing these things? Or who gave you this authority to do them?" 29 Jesus said to them, "I shall ask you one question. Answer me, and I will tell you by what authority I do these things. 30 Was John's baptism of heavenly or of human origin? Answer me." 31 They discussed this among themselves and said, "If we say, 'Of heavenly origin,' he will say, '(Then) why did you not believe him?' 32 But shall we say, 'Of human origin'?"—they feared the crowd, for they all thought John really was a prophet. 33 So they said to Jesus in reply, "We do not know." Then Jesus said to them, "Neither shall I tell you by what authority I do these things."

The last pericope in chapter 11 and all of chapter 12 contain a series of loosely connected stories that take place in the temple area in Jerusalem. These five pronouncement stories and a saying portray Jesus, for the most part, in controversy with various representatives of Judaism. The first of these stories deals with the question about the origin of Jesus' authority. From whom does he get his authority? The chief priests, scribes and elders are trying to trap Jesus into claiming that he received his authority from God. Such an answer would have immediately brought forth the charge of blasphemy (cf. 14:64). Jesus avoids this dilemma by asking his questioners about the source of John the Baptist's authority. Now they have a problem. If they said that John's authority came from heaven, then why had they refused to listen to John? If they denied the divine origin of John's authority, the

145

crowd would have become angry, because they thought John was a prophet. They respond by refusing to take a clear, public stand concerning John.

In asking the question about John, Jesus has paralleled himself with John. The questioners in the Gospel would have realized this, as does the reader of Mark's Gospel. The assumption in Jesus' question is that John's authority is from God; the implied answer, therefore, is that Jesus too gets his power from God. Mark presents Jesus as a powerful teacher and miracle worker, who receives his authority from God. To see anyone else, especially Satan, as the source of his authority would be a very serious error.

Parable of the Tenants (12:1-12)

12:1 He began to speak to them in parables. "A man planted a vineyard, put a hedge around it, dug a wine press, and built a tower. Then he leased it to tenant farmers and left on a journey. 2 At the proper time he sent a servant to the tenants to obtain from them some of the produce of the vineyard. 3 But they seized him, beat him, and sent him away empty-handed. 4 Again he sent them another servant. And that one they beat over the head and treated shamefully. 5 He sent yet another whom they killed. So, too, many others; some they beat, others they killed. 6 He had one other to send, a beloved son. He sent him to them last of all, thinking, 'They will respect my son.' 7 But those tenants said to one another, 'This is the heir. Come, let us kill him, and the inheritance will be ours.' 8 So they seized him and killed him, and threw him out of the vineyard. 9 What (then) will the owner of the vineyard do? He will come, put the tenants to death, and give the vineyard to others. 10 Have you not read this scripture passage: 'The stone that the builders rejected has become the cornerstone; [11] by the Lord has this been done, and it is wonderful in our eyes'?" [12] They were seeking to arrest him, but they feared the crowd, for they realized that he had addressed the parable to them. So they left him and went away.

The parable of the tenants is one which contains some obvious allegorical allusions. The vineyard should be seen as Israel (cf. Is 5:1-7). The tenant farmers are the religious leaders of Israel to whom God, the owner of the vineyard, sends messengers (i.e., the prophets). The heir, the beloved son, is Jesus (cf. Mk 1:11; 9:7). The others to whom the vineyard was transferred probably refers to the people of the new covenant, since Jesus was welcomed more by Gentiles than by Jews. Mark's claim is that Israel's rejection of the prophets reached a climax by its murder of Jesus. The inclusion of Psalm 118:22-23 in this pericope reinforces the point of the parable, namely, that in rejecting Jesus the Jewish leaders have made a terrible mistake. The contrast here is between the rebellious Israel and the mercy of God, who sends his Son. God's response to human sin is forgiving love or mercy.

It is natural to wonder if this trajectory of the rejection of God's messengers ended with the death of Jesus or continued on after his death. Mark's emphasis on the suffering of Jesus throughout his Gospel suggests that Mark understands suffering to be an integral part of the life of a disciple. This passage implies that whenever God's messengers speak to the world on God's behalf they are persecuted and often killed. The suffering experienced by the prophets and Jesus has continued throughout the centuries. Christians who carry the message of Jesus to the world should not be surprised if they are discriminated against or suffer physically or materially. This was the experience of the martyrs in the early Church and in recent Church history. Mention of the murder of Archbishop Oscar Romero in El Salvador in 1980 should bring to mind the names of countless other Christians whose public witness to their faith has caused suffering and death. Martin Luther King, Jr., is often cited as someone who stood up for gospel values and paid for it with suffering and death.

For reflection: Do you believe that suffering is to be expected as you attempt to live your life in accordance with the teachings of Jesus? What is your attitude toward the world in which we live? Do you believe that if Jesus came again and delivered his message to the world of the twenty-first century, he would be killed again? Have you protested injustice whenever you have seen it, or have you made excuses which led to a lack of involvement? Have you too easily embraced the values of the world? Is there something happening in your business or in your neighborhood that cries out for support or demands a challenge in light of Jesus' teachings? Have you spoken up?

Taxes to Caesar (12:13-17)

13 They sent some Pharisees and Herodians to him to ensnare him in his speech. 14 They came and said to him, "Teacher, we know that you are a truthful man and that you are not concerned with anyone's opinion. You do not regard a person's status but teach the way of God in accordance with the truth. Is it lawful to pay the census tax to Caesar or not? Should we pay or should we not pay?" 15 Knowing their hypocrisy he said to them, "Why are you testing me? Bring me a denarius to look at."

¹⁶They brought one to him and he said to them, "Whose image and inscription is this?" They replied to him, "Caesar's." ¹⁷ So Jesus said to them, "Repay to Caesar what belongs to Caesar and to God what belongs to God." They were utterly amazed at him.

This story has been cited by some in the modern world as support for paying taxes and joining the military and by others for not paying taxes and not joining the military. What is its function in this section of Mark's Gospel?

As in the previous pericope, Jesus' opponents are trying to put him in a double bind. It is impossible to give an answer that will get him out of the dilemma. If he says that one should pay taxes, the crowds will be furious. The coin which Jesus asks his opponents to produce is a Roman denarius, which had on it not only Caesar's likeness but also the inscription "Tiberius Caesar, Augustus, son of divine Augustus." Such a coin was a serious affront to the Jewish nationalist sensibilities. In addition, Roman taxes were seen as an oppressive burden by the Jews. Jewish tax collectors who worked for the Romans were regarded as sinners, outcasts of society, and disgraced along with their families, because they extorted money from their co-religionists on behalf of the Roman government. If Jesus had urged his questioners to pay these taxes, he would have been seen as a traitor by the Jews. On the other hand, if Jesus had counseled tax resistance, he would have been viewed as a traitor by the Roman authorities. By rejecting Roman taxation, Jesus would have made himself liable to arrest and trial for inciting a rebellion.

Jesus escapes this trap by giving a response that answers, yet does not really answer, the question. He exposes the hypocrisy of his opponents when he asks them for, and they produce, a denarius (the Roman coin used to pay the poll tax). These supposedly sincere questioners are apparently willing to carry and use Caesar's money in their daily business activities. In this light, then, Jesus says they should give back to Caesar what is his. Although Jesus allows them to pay the poll tax, his reasoning suggests that this is merely a case of giving back to Caesar what was already his. By adding that they should give "to God what belongs to God" (12:17), Jesus reminds his audience that they also have obligations to God. He challenges them to be as conscientious in fulfilling their commitments to God as they apparently are in fulfilling their responsibilities to Caesar. In effect, he accuses his opponents of not paying God what is due to God.

For reflection: This pericope causes most modern readers to reflect on the current tax system and Church-State relations. While this is probably well beyond what the Markan context would bear, it is a fair question for those trying to live a Christian life in a different cultural situation than Mark faced. What is really being asked is whether the requirements for "being a good citizen" and "being a good Christian" are identical. Can your obligations to the state and your obligations to God ever come into conflict? If they ever do, is it obvious that your obligations to God take precedence?

The Sadducees and the Resurrection (12:18-27)

[18] Some Sadducees, who say there is no resurrection, came to him and put this question to him, [19] saying, "Teacher, Moses wrote for us, 'If someone's brother dies, leaving a wife but no child, his brother must take

the wife and raise up descendants for his brother.'
[20] Now there were seven brothers. The first married a woman and died, leaving no descendants. [21] So the second married her and died, leaving no descendants, and the third likewise. [22] And the seven left no descendants. Last of all the woman also died. [23] At the resurrection (when they arise) whose wife will she be? For all seven had been married to her." [24] Jesus said to them, "Are you not misled because you do not know the scriptures or the power of God? [25] When they rise from the dead, they neither marry nor are given in marriage, but they are like the angels in heaven. [26] As for the dead being raised, have you not read in the Book of Moses, in the passage about the bush, how God told him, 'I am the God of Abraham, (the) God of Isaac, and (the) God of Jacob'? [27] He is not God of the dead but of the living. You are greatly misled."

The Sadducees were the aristocratic and priestly group that controlled the temple and its lands. They rejected the Pharisees' position that the oral tradition was on a par with written scripture, and they refused to accept as normative any doctrine that they perceived as not contained in the Pentateuch or Torah (the first five books of the Hebrew Bible). For this same reason, they denied the resurrection of the dead.

The reference to what Moses wrote (Moses was thought to be the author of the Pentateuch) is a citation from Deuteronomy 25:5-10 dealing with levirate marriage. Because they did not have a developed idea of an afterlife, the early Israelites sought a type of afterlife in their descendants. It was essential that a male produce a male offspring to carry on the family name and inherit the family property. The Deuteronomy text holds that if a man dies without having produced a male heir it is the responsibility of his brother

151

to marry the widow and produce a male child. The child born from this union would bear the name of the dead man and be considered his legal heir. The implicit argument of the Sadducees in this pericope seems to be that the Pentateuch would not have gone to such lengths in requiring a man to "continue the line of the deceased brother" (Dt 25:6) if there was another form of immortality.

The example these Sadducees use in their exchange with Jesus suggests that they understand the term resurrection to mean a return to the conditions and relationships enjoyed in ordinary, everyday life. If there was a resurrection, then the resurrected life would be an idealized version of life as we know it. This leads them to ask which of the woman's seven husbands would be her husband for eternity.

Jesus answers their challenge by accusing them of understanding neither the scriptures nor the power of God. In explaining the nature of the resurrection, Jesus says that their conception of what resurrected life will be like is entirely wrong. The kind of relationships we experience in this world will be transcended; there will be a new kind of existence in the afterlife (12:25).

In his response to their scriptural claims, Jesus argues in a way that is consistent with accepted methods of rabbinical exegesis (scriptural interpretation) in the first century. His task here is to demonstrate to the Sadducees that the doctrine of the resurrection is found in the Pentateuch. Jesus does this by citing the famous passage about the appearance of Yahweh to Moses in the burning bush (Ex 3:6, 15-16). Yahweh is presented as using present tense verbs to describe his relationship with the long dead

Abraham, Isaac and Jacob. If Yahweh can say "I am" the God of Abraham, the God of Isaac, and the God of Jacob, and not "I was" or "I used to be," then he must have a continuing relationship with these patriarchs; they must still be alive. This could only be the case if there is an afterlife.

People have speculated on the resurrected life for well over two millennia. Oftentimes the assumption implicit in this pericope, that the afterlife is a bigger and better version of life as we experience it now, is the belief that directs the conversation. A variety of solutions have been suggested. Perhaps the most famous is the one suggesting that we will appear as we looked or would have looked at the perfect age (i.e., at thirty-three, the age Jesus was said to have been when he was crucified).

For reflection: Does this mean that all speculation about the afterlife is pointless? Is it enough to conclude that God, who had the power to create everything in the beginning (12:24), has the power to recreate it after death?

Love of God and Love of Neighbor (12:28-34)

28 One of the scribes, when he came forward and heard them disputing and saw how well he had answered them, asked him, "Which is the first of all the commandments?" 29 Jesus replied, "The first is this: 'Hear, O Israel! The Lord our God is Lord alone! 30 You shall love the Lord your God with all your heart, with all your soul, with all your mind, and with all your strength.' 31 The second is this: 'You shall love your neighbor as yourself.' There is no other commandment greater than these." 32 The scribe said to him, "Well said, teacher. You are right in saying, 'He is One and there is no other than he.' 33 And 'to love him with all your heart, with all your

understanding, with all your strength, and to love your neighbor as yourself' is worth more than all burnt offerings and sacrifices." [34] And when Jesus saw that (he) answered with understanding, he said to him, "You are not far from the kingdom of God." And no one dared to ask him any more questions.

Mark next presents the only passage in his Gospel in which a scribe has a positive attitude toward Jesus. The suggestion would be that not all orthodox Jews rejected Jesus. The two commandments mentioned here are the foundation of Jewish law (cf. Dt 6:4-5; Lv 19:18) and the basis of New Testament ethics. All other commandments, rules, and regulations take their life from them. Insofar as any rule helps you to love God and love your neighbor as yourself, it is a good law. Insofar as any regulation hinders you in your quest to love God completely and to love your neighbor as yourself, it is a bad law. These two commandments indicate that one's love of God must be demonstrated in concrete acts of love toward one's neighbor. All acts must be rooted in these two commandments.

Oftentimes it is the second commandment which Jesus mentions that causes individuals the most difficulty. The requirement to love God completely, with all your heart, soul, mind, and strength, is sometimes seen as too abstract to be succinctly defined. Many find it easy to convince themselves that they do, in fact, fulfill this commandment. The injunction to love one's neighbor in the same way that one loves oneself, however, is seen as altogether too concrete. Love of neighbor implies an absolute demand for justice, namely a recognition of the dignity and rights of one's neighbor. We are called to care about our neighbor with the same intensity that we care about ourselves. The Christian, therefore, can be said to have a duty to proclaim justice on the social, national, and international level, and to denounce instances of injustice, whenever the defense of fundamental human rights demands it.

For reflection: Is Jesus suggesting a profoundly non-legalistic understanding of Christian morality? Are rules and regulations to be viewed not as absolutes but as guidelines? When contemplating any action, is the only important question whether or not it is consistent with loving God and loving one's neighbor as oneself? Are we talking here about an act of conscience in which the individual judges a specific act to be morally right or wrong based on whether it helps or hinders one's love of God and one's neighbor? Authentic love is courageous, takes initiative, and can be costly both socially and economically. Do you conduct your life in a way that would be consistent with this understanding of the commandment to love your neighbor as yourself?

The Son of David, the Scribes and the Widow (12:35-44)

[35] As Jesus was teaching in the temple area he said, "How do the scribes claim that the Messiah is the son of David? [36] David himself, inspired by the Holy Spirit, said: 'The Lord said to my lord, "Sit at my right hand until I place your enemies under your feet."' [37] David himself calls him 'lord'; so how is he his son?" (The) great crowd heard this with delight. [38] In the course of his teaching he said, "Beware of the scribes, who like to go around in long robes and accept greetings in the market-places, [39] seats of honor in synagogues, and places of

honor at banquets. [40] They devour the houses of widows and, as a pretext, recite lengthy prayers. They will receive a very severe condemnation." [41] He sat down opposite the treasury and observed how the crowd put money into the treasury. Many rich people put in large sums. [42] A poor widow also came and put in two small coins worth a few cents. [43] Calling his disciples to himself, he said to them, "Amen, I say to you, this poor widow put in more than all the other contributors to the treasury. [44] For they have all contributed from their surplus wealth, but she, from her poverty, has contributed all she had, her whole livelihood."

In the first part of this passage, Jesus disputes a specific point of scribal teaching (12:35-37); in the second, he warns against imitating the behavior of the scribes (12:38-44). Jesus seems to be contesting the teaching of the scribes when he asks, "How do the scribes claim that the Messiah is the son of David?" Mark's aim in these verses is to indicate that Jesus the Messiah is more than just the Son of David. It is assumed that David is the author of Psalm 110, which is cited in 12:36. Therefore when David speaks about the Messiah as "my lord" he implies that the Messiah is someone different from himself. According to Mark, the Messiah is superior to David and to any son fathered by David. Mark's christological concerns are apparent again.

The last two passages of chapter 12 contrast the actions of the scribes and the poor widow. Jesus warns his disciples against imitating the fondness of the scribes for long robes, for greetings of respect from people in the marketplaces, for seats of honor in the synagogues, and for places of privilege at banquets. All of this is a fraud and pretense, which should not be part of a disciple's way of life. The scribes, interpreters of the Jewish law (i.e., ancient Jewish lawyers), were probably using these long robes to enhance their prestige. They saw themselves as important religious dignitaries who deserved the applause and respect of the common people. A similar motivation is seen in their desire to occupy seats of honor in the synagogue and at feasts. In the synagogue, the best seats were on the platform facing the congregation. These scribes would have sat at the front facing the people so that everyone could see and admire them. At feasts they apparently rushed for the distinguished positions on the right-hand side of the host. Jesus indicates that such maneuvering for prestigious chairs is not how his disciples should be behaving.

Early rabbinic custom required that a greeting between people be initiated by the one inferior in the knowledge of the law. Apparently these scribes enjoyed the reinforcement of their social standing that was an integral part of such greetings. In his critique of these prestige-seeking scribes, Jesus rejects status seeking and their desire to continually call attention to status differences. The scribes presume to pass themselves off as important, yet they are the ones who devour the little that widows have left. They cover up such activity with the appearance of religious piety, saying lengthy prayers to God (probably for the sake of social display).

The story of the widow's offering which follows, is best seen as a negative example of the scribes' way of thinking. This interpretation might come as a surprise to some readers, who are used to seeing this story as a lesson about giving according to one's means or giving in the proper spirit. But nothing is said about the interior motive of the widow. According to Mark, she does not give according to her means but well beyond her means. It would be a mistake to see Jesus praising her actions in this case.

In our earlier comments on Mark 7:10-13, we concluded that Jesus believed human needs to take precedence over certain religious values when they conflict. We reached a similar conclusion discussing Jesus' healings on the sabbath (e.g., 3:1-5). It would seem inconsistent, therefore, to conclude that in the story of the widow Jesus was enthusiastic about the fact that she "contributed all she had, her whole livelihood" (12:44).

Widows are the stereotypical symbol of the exploited and oppressed in Hebrew society. The position of a widow was one of extreme vulnerability. The widow had no inheritance rights to her husband's property. When her husband died it was the eldest son who acquired the property rights. If there was no son, she might be married to her brother-in-law in a levirate marriage (mentioned above) or return to her father's house (Lv 22:13; Ru 1:8). In a male-dominated society, widows (like other women) did not speak on their own behalf and had no role in public or religious life.

The present context of this pericope suggests that the widow's actions are directly related to Jesus' condemnation of the scribes, who "devour the houses of widows" (12:40). Her religious thinking is attributed to the teaching of the scribes. She has been taught and encouraged to donate all that she had. Jesus is lamenting, not praising, her actions. He condemns the religious system that motivates her to think that her actions in this instance are appropriate and pleasing to God.

For reflection: These stories invite us to reflect on our atti-

158

tude toward charitable contributions. How much is too much? If you are, or have been, in a position to influence others in this regard, how careful have you been in your eagerness to increase donations? Have you said things which have caused others to conclude that they had to contribute at a level far beyond their means? There is probably a widow in your faith community whose level of giving has not changed even though her husband has died and her income has dropped. While it is true that some individuals could afford to donate more, it is also true that some should be contributing less. Is this a message that members of your faith community hear from you?

Jesus' Apocalyptic Discourse (13:1-37)

> ¹³:¹ As he was making his way out of the temple area one of his disciples said to him, "Look, teacher, what stones and what buildings!" ² Jesus said to him, "Do you see these great buildings? There will not be one stone left upon another that will not be thrown down." ³ As he was sitting on the Mount of Olives opposite the temple area, Peter, James, John, and Andrew asked him privately, ⁴ "Tell us, when will this happen, and what sign will there be when all these things are about to come to an end?"

After finishing his work in the temple area, Jesus and his disciples move on to the Mount of Olives where Jesus delivers his second major discourse in Mark's Gospel. The first two verses of chapter 13 have Jesus predicting the temple's downfall (foreshadowed already in the fig tree story, 11:12-14, 20-26). The next two verses find Jesus seated on the Mount of Olives opposite the temple where he will deliver his apocalyptic speech. Although in its present context this speech could be seen as addressed only to Peter, James, John, and Andrew (13:3-4), it is clear that Mark intended his readers to see themselves included in the "all" of the final verse: "What I say to you, I say to all: 'Watch!'" (13:37). The setting is dramatic because of the eschatological connotations in Zechariah 14:4 (mentioned above) and because the Mount of Olives is approximately ninety feet higher than the temple mount. Thus, Jesus is pictured as looking down on the temple as he predicts its destruction.

Mark 13 has often been called the "little apocalypse." Apocalyptic literature is designed to comfort readers during a time of distress (e.g., persecution, exile). It reveals to them the fact that this period of trouble is part of God's plan, and it explains what is to be expected in the near future, before God intervenes to bring the present evils to an end. Jewish apocalyptic literature is dualistic; it speaks about the present evil age, characterized by trials and tribulations, and the glorious age to come. It holds that at some future moment God will intervene and bring history as we know it to an end. Evil will be annihilated and those who are righteous will be saved. This future, idyllic age provides hope to those who find themselves oppressed by the forces of evil in the present world. Usually the intended reader and the author are thought to be living in the final days of this present evil age. The message is both a promise and a warning that the intervention of God is about to happen. Longer biblical examples of apocalyptic writing are found in the Book of Daniel and in the Book of Revelation (Apocalypse of John).

In involved and highly figurative language, the author communicates a message of perseverance or resistance to those who understand the imagery. The immediate crisis is seen as a crucial stage in the final conflict between God and the powers of evil; therefore the emphasis is on preparing for the end and final judgment. Steadfastness leads to complete victory in which God's purpose for creation will be achieved. The focus of New Testament apocalyptic literature, thus, is primarily ethical.

Jesus' apocalyptic speech is divided into three parts: comments on past and present history (13:5b-23), the parousia (13:24-27), and the nearness of the parousia (13:28-37). In the first part of the discourse, Jesus indicates that the end-time has not yet arrived; the present signs should be seen as preliminary. This section of the speech begins and ends with references to false Christs (13:6, 22). Mark's intercalation technique might be at work here. In between these references to false Messiahs are comments about wars, earthquakes and famines (13:7-8), persecutions (13:9-13), and the "desolating abomination" and suffering (13:14-21). The setting and introduction show that expectations of the second coming of Christ were related in some way to the destruction of the temple.

⁵Jesus began to say to them, "See that no one deceives you. ⁶Many will come in my name saying, 'I am he,' and they will deceive many. ⁷When you hear of wars and reports of wars do not be alarmed; such things must happen, but it will not yet be the end. ⁸Nation will rise against nation and kingdom against kingdom. There will be earthquakes from place to place and there will be famines. These are the beginnings of the labor pains. ⁹Watch out for yourselves. They will hand you over to the courts. You will be beaten in synagogues. You will be arraigned before governors and kings because of me, as a witness before them. ¹⁰But the gospel must first be

preached to all nations. [11] When they lead you away and hand you over, do not worry beforehand about what you are to say. But say whatever will be given to you at that hour. For it will not be you who are speaking but the Holy Spirit. [12] Brother will hand over brother to death, and the father his child; children will rise up against parents and have them put to death. [13] You will be hated by all because of my name. But the one who perseveres to the end will be saved."

Jesus begins this discourse by warning his audience not to be disturbed by reports of wars, earthquakes, or other disasters and not to be led astray by religious pretenders. He is urging a cautious, hope-filled waiting rather than the eschatological urgency and frantic activity usually found in false messianic movements like those incited by zealots. These revolutionaries commonly saw themselves as initiating events that would bring ordinary world history as we know it to a close. These enthusiastic and alarmist movements are not to be believed. In his first discourse (4:3ff.) Jesus told his followers that God was in charge of the timetable, and the hidden kingdom had to go through stages before it would be revealed in its fullness. He urged his followers not to despair if some people fell away because of persecution, worldly anxiety, or the lure of riches (4:17-19). Here Jesus presents a similar message. Do not be led astray by those claiming that Christ has returned, that the parousia has already occurred. Do not despair at news of natural or human created disasters. What is required is hope and trust that God is ultimately in control of world history and will bring it to a close according to God's own timetable.

In 13:10, Jesus states that the end will not come until the gospel has been "preached to all nations." This looks forward to the Christian mission to the Gentiles, which will take place in earnest only after the resurrection of Jesus. How much this slows down the eschatological time-table is open to question. It explains why the parousia has not occurred during the forty years between the death of Jesus and the writing of Mark's Gospel. It is likely, how-ever, that Mark understands the spread of the gospel during these forty years very nearly to fulfill the require-ment that the good news be preached to all nations. There is convincing evidence that Mark thought of the parousia as imminent (cf. 13:28-37). What he urges in the time remaining is faithful, patient endurance (13:13).

> [14] "When you see the desolating abomination stand-ing where he should not (let the reader understand), then those in Judea must flee to the mountains, [15] (and) a person on a housetop must not go down or enter to get anything out of his house, [16] and a person in a field must not return to get his cloak. [17] Woe to pregnant women and nursing mothers in those days. [18] Pray that this does not happen in winter. [19] For those times will have tribu-lation such as has not been since the beginning of God's creation until now, nor ever will be. [20] If the Lord had not shortened those days, no one would be saved; but for the sake of the elect whom he chose, he did shorten the days."

Among Jesus' words about the great tribulation is a ref-erence to the "desolating abomination" (13:14). This expression is taken from the Book of Daniel (9:27; 11:3; 12:11) where it refers to the setting up in 168 B.C.E. of an altar to Zeus in the Jerusalem temple by the king of Syria, Antiochus IV Epiphanes. Here in Mark 13 it most likely refers to the Roman destruction of Jerusalem and its temple in 70 C.E. God has established a timetable for the coming of the kingdom (cf. Mk 13:20), and there is a connection between the destruction of the Jerusalem temple and the parousia. The preliminary signs have taken place and Mark tells his readers that when they see these things happening they should realize that the parousia is near (cf. 13:29).

After these preliminary signs take place the end will come, and no one will be able to miss it because of the cosmic signs that will accompany it. The emphasis is on the open, public character of the parousia, in order to discredit those individuals or groups that claim the Messiah has already returned. Jesus speaks about these cosmic disturbances (13:24-25), the Son of Man coming in glory (13:26), and the elect being gathered together (13:27). The reader learns that the end is coming soon, within the present generation (13:28-31), and is warned that no one is capable of calculating the exact time of the Son of Man's return. The end is certain and near, yet will be sudden and unexpected. What is required is watchful, prayerful waiting (13:32-36). The entire chapter ends with the admonition, "Watch!"

Mark seems to be concerned with the problem of premature claims that Christ has come again (13:6, 21-22). The comment in verse 22, that these false messiahs and false prophets will perform signs and wonders in order to mislead, is further indication of the ambiguity inherent in miracles. While Mark is at considerable pains to counter the idea that the parousia has already occurred, or is about to, he is also intent on assuring his readers that it will come in the near future. There is danger in premature expectations, but there is an equal or greater danger in ceasing to look for Christ altogether. Warnings against premature claims about the parousia are seen together with admonitions to be alert, for it is coming in the near future.

Although New Testament apocalyptic literature is primarily ethical, in our modern world some people spend less time discussing eschatology and ethics and most of the time trying to figure out the timetable for the last days. They take highly symbolic material from Daniel and New Testament apocalyptic literature and give it literal and culturally biased interpretations in order to interpret complex events and explain when and how the world will end. This should not surprise us. Since the Church began, some people out of either their struggle or their theology have expected the imminent return of Christ. Modern scholarship suggests that popular eschatology begins with the wrong question: What is the timetable of the last days, when Christ will return to set up his kingdom? In Mark 13:32, Jesus indicates that as to the exact day or hour, "no one knows, neither the angels in heaven, nor the Son, but only the Father." The nearness of the parousia must not tempt Christians to engage in speculation and calculation about the precise date of the second coming. We must recognize that biblical eschatology is primarily ethical and only secondarily predictive. A better question to ask would be, What does God desire for the human future? This would allow us to approach the future with hope, not fatalism.

From its beginning, the Christian community looked forward eagerly to a time when God would complete the work of transforming creation. This hopefulness and expectancy is strong in the prophetic tradition. Jesus announced that the kingdom of God was at hand, and the early Church prayed for the coming of the kingdom. New Testament writers agreed that God would establish a new age; as to when, where, and how, there is no such agreement.

For reflection: Do you believe that the second coming of the Messiah has already taken place? Do you believe that Christ will come again in the future to judge the living and the dead? Do you live as if this could occur at any time, a time when you least expect it?

> [21] "If anyone says to you then, 'Look, here is the Messiah! Look, there he is!' do not believe it. [22] False messiahs and false prophets will arise and will perform signs and wonders in order to mislead, if that were possible, the elect. [23] Be watchful! I have told it all to you beforehand."

The world in which we live presents us with numerous false messiahs. They might be political figures, popular musicians, or religious figures. Today, the term "messiah" can be used in a way different than it is in the New Testament. A professed or accepted leader of some hope or cause is often referred to as a messiah. This person, or the related message, is expected to free believers from oppression and establish a right order that will last forever.

For reflection: Most of us are probably aware of modern-day individuals with a message that appears to be liberating and to offer hope to a troubled world. We must ask ourselves if we have been guilty of saying "Look, here is the Messiah! Look, there he is!" (13:21). Do you look for salvation from anyone other than Jesus the Christ, the risen Lord?

²⁴"But in those days after that tribulation the sun will be darkened, and the moon will not give its light, ²⁵ and the stars will be falling from the sky, and the powers in the heavens will be shaken. ²⁶And then they will see 'the Son of Man coming in the clouds' with great power and glory, ²⁷ and then he will send out the angels and gather (his) elect from the four winds, from the end of the earth to the end of the sky. ²⁸ Learn a lesson from the fig tree. When its branch becomes tender and sprouts leaves, you know that summer is near. ²⁹ In the same way, when you see these things happening, know that he is near, at the gates. ³⁰Amen, I say to you, this generation will not pass away until all these things have taken place. ³¹ Heaven and earth will pass away, but my words will not pass away. ³²But of that day or hour, no one knows, neither the angels in heaven, nor the Son, but only the Father. ³³Be watchful! Be alert! You do not know when the time will come. ³⁴ It is like a man traveling abroad. He leaves home and places his servants in charge, each with his work, and orders the gatekeeper to be on the watch. ³⁵Watch, therefore; you do not know when the lord of the house is coming, whether in the evening, or at midnight, or at cockcrow, or in the morning. ³⁶May he not come suddenly and find you sleeping. ³⁷What I say to you, I say to all: 'Watch!'"

If finding false messiahs in the contemporary world is not our problem, we must ask ourselves about our beliefs concerning the second coming of Christ. The so-called delay of the parousia has been a problem for Christians since the first century. The lesson of the fig tree (13:28-31) suggests that the end is not far off. This is the most obvious reading of Jesus' comment, "I say to you, this generation will not pass away until all these things have taken place" (13:30). When one loses this imminent expectation of the end it is easy to become morally lazy or apathetic. The eschatological imperative disappears.

In order for us to appreciate the apocalyptic message of Mark 13, it is sometimes necessary for modern readers to understand this language and imagery as referring to one's own death, not to the end of the world as we know it. This does not appear to be what the New Testament authors had in mind, but it is a useful homiletical tool. Once this shift is made, one can state that it will take place during our lifetime, it will probably be unexpected and sooner that we think. In the interim, however long this will be, we must "Watch!"

For reflection: You probably know one or more individuals who appeared to be the picture of health, yet died suddenly from a heart attack or an automobile accident. Does the realization that you could die today, tomorrow, or the next day motivate you to act morally at all times? Rather than focus on the unknown timetable, do you accept the invitation found in New Testament apocalyptic literature to concentrate on the ethical?

Conclusion

Jesus uses apocalyptic language in speaking vaguely of wars and reports of wars, of nation rising against nation, and of kingdom against kingdom. What the reader must recognize is that these three pairs are standard apocalyptic stage props; they are expected to appear in the apocalyptic literary genre. The apocalyptic world view has a number of distinct characteristics. The modern reader must not take every reference literally. What has survived in the mainline Christian tradition is the belief in the second coming of Christ and in a final judgment. All else is seen as part of the apocalyptic genre.

In a special way, the apocalyptic genre reflected in Mark 13 provides individuals with a sense of belonging to a larger reality and offers a framework for defining a sense of personal meaning. Ultimately, its message is one of hope in the final victory of the good. In this regard it serves to call people to make a decision with respect to good and evil. Jesus promises that endurance in suffering for the sake of the good will be rewarded and warns that persistence in evil will be punished.

VI

The Passion Narrative
(14:1 – 16:8)

The last section of Mark's Gospel chronicles the final days of Jesus in Jerusalem. It begins two days before the Passover and the Feast of the Unleavened Bread, and ends with the story about the women at the empty tomb. There are no surprises here, as the reader finds the fulfillment of Jesus' predictions that his words will not pass away (13:31) and that he told all beforehand (13:23).

Plans to Kill Jesus (14:1-2)

[1] The Passover and the Feast of Unleavened Bread were to take place in two days' time. So the chief priests and the scribes were seeking a way to arrest him by treachery and put him to death. [2] They said, "Not during the festival, for fear that there may be a riot among the people."

Chapter 14 begins with the chief priests and scribes plotting to kill Jesus. Mark, on the whole, tends to blame the *leaders* of the Jews and to present the people as misled or misdirected. The authorities want to arrest Jesus, but they fear a riot among the multitudes who are in Jerusalem to celebrate the Passover.

On the afternoon of the fourteenth of Nisan the Passover lamb was sacrificed. That evening (now the fifteenth of Nisan, since the Jewish day begins at sundown) the Passover meal was celebrated. This meal was celebrated on the evening of the first full moon of Spring. The feast of Unleavened Bread (which served as a reminder of the night that marked the end of Israel's oppression in Egypt) began on the fifteenth of Nisan and lasted seven days. Both springtime feasts commemorate God's liberation of the Israelite people from Egypt.

The Passover context for the Last Supper (14:22ff.) was determinative for the shape of the Christian liturgical year. Most scholars believe that an annual observance of the death of Jesus was celebrated by the primitive Christian community from the very beginning. The Exodus images of liberation, covenant, and redemption, combined with the sacrificial and memorial rites that comprised the Jewish Passover celebration of the first century, would have provided a rich setting for the remembrance of the death of Jesus. The Council of Nicea (325 C.E.) declared that the Christian Passover (Easter) should be celebrated on the Sunday following the first full moon after the vernal equinox (about March 21).

Jesus in Bethany (14:3-11)

[3] When he was in Bethany reclining at table in the house of Simon the leper, a woman came with an alabaster jar of perfumed oil, costly genuine spikenard. She broke the alabaster jar and poured it on his head. [4] There were some who were indignant. "Why has there been this waste of perfumed oil? [5] It could have been sold for more than three hundred days' wages and the money given to the poor." They were infuriated with her. [6] Jesus said, "Let her alone. Why do you make trouble for her?

171

She has done a good thing for me. ⁷ The poor you will always have with you, and whenever you wish you can do good to them, but you will not always have me. ⁸ She has done what she could. She has anticipated anointing my body for burial. ⁹ Amen, I say to you, wherever the gospel is proclaimed to the whole world, what she has done will be told in memory of her." ¹⁰ Then Judas Iscariot, one of the Twelve, went off to the chief priests to hand him over to them. ¹¹ When they heard him they were pleased and promised to pay him money. Then he looked for an opportunity to hand him over.

In this pericope, the reader finds Jesus in Bethany at the home of Simon the leper. The theological importance of this story is that it is directed toward the burial of Jesus (14:8). At the beginning of the passion narrative, therefore, we again encounter the theme of Jesus' messiahship that includes suffering and death. Jesus is sitting at the table in the house of Simon the leper when an unnamed woman pours costly ointment over Jesus' head. We soon learn that she has performed an act of prophetic anticipation, because she has anointed his body "for burial" (14:8). This is the only anointing Jesus receives, since the women who come to the tomb to anoint his corpse discover that he has already risen (16:1-6).

Immediately after this obvious reference to the death of Jesus, we find another disciple who fails to understand, or refuses to accept, that Jesus must suffer and die. Judas Iscariot goes to the chief priests in order to betray Jesus to them (14:10-11). There are at least two possible ways to understand this: (1) Mark might want the reader to see Judas as so preoccupied with his own concerns that he fails to comprehend what has just happened. Thus, Judas' reaction to the announcement of Jesus' impending death would be similar to the disciples' reaction following the second and third passion-resurrection predictions. (2) Mark might want the reader to see in Judas someone who comprehends, at least partially, the meaning of the anointing and rejects this understanding of messiahship. Thus, Judas' reaction would be similar to that of Peter after the first passion-resurrection prediction. In either case, once again we have the mention of Jesus' death followed by a less than acceptable reaction by one of his closest followers.

In having this woman anoint Jesus' head, Mark is suggesting that she recognized Jesus as the Messiah (cf. 2 Kgs 9:6). This calls to mind our earlier conclusion that Mark portrays the least likely individuals as recognizing who Jesus really is, while those closest to him and the religious authorities do not recognize him.

In examining the figure of Judas in this Gospel, one must be careful not to read in material from other gospels. Mark does not give any motivation for Judas' act. It seems clear, however, that Judas did not hand Jesus over to the authorities for the money, since verse 11 indicates that only after Judas spoke with them did the chief priests promise to pay him money.

We must also reflect on Jesus' words in 14:7: "The poor you will always have with you, and whenever you wish you can do good to them, but you will not always have me." This could lead us to understand that Jesus desires poverty to remain a permanent social problem. Is he suggesting that one not come to the aid of the poor? Is he asking that we construct an economic system so that there will always be poor? This would not seem to be the best reading of this verse given Jesus' teaching elsewhere and the probability that this text would have reminded the original audience of Deuteronomy 15:11: "The needy will never be lacking in the land; that is why I command you to open your hand to your poor and needy kinsman in your country." God's will is expressed earlier in that chapter: "There should be no one of you in need" (Dt 15:4). The fact that there are poor in the land is a result of greed and selfishness. The observation that greed and ambition will probably continue to govern the lives of people and their social systems should not be misread as a justification for the perpetuation of such injustices. The intent of this saying is obviously not that poverty is inevitable and therefore not something to be overly concerned about.

Perhaps the point is that Jesus will die soon and therefore deserves this special honor, while the poor will always be available as objects of charity? Is he implying that once he has died and we cannot anoint his body, we should come to the aid of the poor? In this interpretation the post-resurrection disciple would render service to Jesus by serving the poor, reminiscent of the requirement found in the second and third discipleship discourses, to be "servant of all" (9:35) or "slave of all" (10:44).

The Passover (14:12-21)

In the following scene, Mark sets the stage for his version of the last supper that Jesus shared with his most intimate followers. This final Passover meal that Jesus celebrated with his disciples is composed of four scenes. As the feast approaches, Jesus, acting with great authority, directs his disciples to prepare the Passover (14:12-16). The solemn moment of the meal itself (14:22-26) is surrounded by predictions of betrayal, desertion and denial (14:17-21; 14:27-31).

> [12] On the first day of the Feast of Unleavened Bread, when they sacrificed the Passover lamb, his disciples said to him, "Where do you want us to go and prepare for you to eat the Passover?" [13] He sent two of his disciples and said to them, "Go into the city and a man will meet you, carrying a jar of water. Follow him. [14] Wherever he enters, say to the master of the house, 'The Teacher says, "Where is my guest room where I may eat the Passover with my disciples?"' [15] Then he will show you a large upper room furnished and ready. Make the preparations for us there." [16] The disciples then went off, entered the city, and found it just as he had told them; and they prepared the Passover.

The Feast of the Unleavened Bread (14:12) was the designation for the festival that coincided with Passover. On Thursday Jewish households would have thrown out all leavened bread so that they could properly celebrate the Passover (cf. Ex 12:15). The feast itself would not actually begin until sundown on Thursday. By identifying this as a Passover meal, Mark has drawn a connection between Jesus' impending death and the great Passover themes of sacrifice and liberation. Jesus is about to celebrate his own Passover.

> [17] When it was evening, he came with the Twelve. [18] And as they reclined at table and were eating, Jesus said, "Amen, I say to you, one of you will betray me, one who is eating with me." [19] They began to be distressed and to say to him, one by one, "Surely it is not I?" [20] He said to them, "One of the Twelve, the one who dips with me into the dish. [21] For the Son of Man indeed goes, as it

is written of him, but woe to that man by whom the Son of Man is betrayed. It would be better for that man if he had never been born."

After sundown the feast of Passover begins and Jesus and his disciples enter the city to celebrate the Passover meal.

A startling contrast is made between Jesus and his disciples. Judas betrays a friend into the hands of those who will kill him, Peter will deny ever having known Jesus, and the rest of the male disciples will desert Jesus in his hour of need. Writing at a time when Christians are still subject to persecution, Mark is suggesting that in times of trouble one should emulate Jesus, not his disciples. To hand over a friend to the authorities is a very serious matter. Likewise, to publicly deny Jesus or to flee at the first sign of trouble is not behavior Mark would recommend for his readers.

The same is true today. Jesus has called upon his followers to lead a life of service to others, realizing that such a life will probably include persecution and suffering. We must, therefore, have courage in the face of adversity. We must model our behavior after the female disciples of Jesus, who stood by Jesus and were present at the crucifixion (15:40), and not after the male disciples, who "left him and fled" (14:50). We must not act like Peter and deny knowing Jesus, deny that we are Christians.

For reflection: In much of the world today, freely admitting that one is a Christian will not lead to torture and death, but it might lead to some form of discrimination or ridicule. Is it still possible to be tempted as Peter was? Have you ever found yourself in a situation where the easiest thing to do was to simply deny that you are a Christian?

Christians today also face the temptation of betraying friends. Friendship in the modern world, as at the time of Jesus, often involves table-fellowship as a reality and symbol of social cohesion and shared values. Friendship is a rather intimate relationship. We know more about our friends than about mere acquaintances. This means that they have placed a great deal of trust in us. It is quite easy to betray a friend. It is enough to reveal an intimate detail about a friend to someone who will use it to that friend's disadvantage. Spreading the truth about someone is immensely more harmful than spreading lies. In theory one can prove that a lie is in fact untrue. If the rumor is true, one can only deny it with a lie. Presumably what has been revealed will soon be found out to be true.

By citing Psalm 41:10 ("Even my friend, who had my trust and partook of my bread, has raised his heel against me") in 14:18 and stating that the "Son of Man indeed goes, as it is written of him" (14:21), Mark is suggesting that these events are part of God's plan and not merely an unfortunate accident. This should not, however, be used as an excuse for personal responsibility. The second part of verse 21 indicates that the inevitable fulfillment of prophecy does not absolve Judas from his actions.

For reflection: Your friends have put their reputations, their futures, in your hands. Have you ever been in a situation where you risked handing a friend over to those who would persecute him or her?

The Eucharist (14:22-26)

> [22] While they were eating, he took bread, said the blessing, broke it, and gave it to them, and said, "Take it; this is my body." [23] Then he took a cup, gave thanks, and gave it to them, and they all drank from it. [24] He said to them, "This is my blood of the covenant, which will be shed for many. [25] Amen, I say to you, I shall not drink again the fruit of the vine until the day when I drink it new in the kingdom of God." [26] Then, after singing a hymn, they went out to the Mount of Olives.

Jesus' actions and words at the Passover meal are the heart of this section of the passion narrative. During the meal Jesus takes bread, blesses it, breaks and distributes it to the disciples. He also blesses and distributes the cup. These ritual gestures recall the two feeding stories earlier in the Gospel, one in Jewish territory and one among the Gentiles, where Jesus had taken a small amount and miraculously fed the multitudes (6:34-44; 8:1-9). As mentioned earlier, for Mark's readers these events would have recalled God's miraculous feeding of the people with the manna during their exodus through the desert and the multiplication of food for those in need by Elijah (1 Kgs 17) and Elisha (2 Kgs 4:42-44). The feedings are also symbolic of the future hope of Israel exemplified by the great messianic banquet expected at the end time (cf. Is 26:6-9).

As the meal is being eaten, Jesus performs a prophetic symbolic action that proclaims the meaning of his forthcoming death. The words interpreting the cup are the most explicit. The cup has already been used as a symbol of Jesus' death in the discussion with the sons of Zebedee after the third passion-resurrection prediction (10:38-39) and will be used again in this way in the Gethsemane scene (14:36).

The cup of wine is interpreted in Mark in terms of covenant blood. This is an allusion to the sacrifice that concluded the Sinai Covenant in Exodus 24:5-8. Jesus' whole life is a sacrifice poured out to create a new community of life, a new covenant between God and the followers of Jesus. The comment that Jesus' blood will be "shed for many" (12:24) is a reference to Isaiah 53:12, one of the Suffering Servant passages. When Mark casts Jesus in the role of the Suffering Servant, who will "give his life as a ransom for many" (10:45), he is using sacrificial terminology. The Servant was expected to atone for the sins of the world by bearing them. Here at the last supper, Mark presents Jesus as ratifying in his blood a covenant bond between God and human beings. This signifies a relationship of friendship and obedience, which is based upon forgiveness, redemption and reconciliation. Mark's focus here is probably on discipleship as well as christology. The disciples are reminded of the importance of service as Mark reveals Jesus' identity as the Suffering Servant, a model for the disciples to follow. Just as Jesus told them to take up their crosses after the first passion-resurrection prediction (8:34) so he tells them to be servants of all after the second (9:35) and slaves of all after the third (10:44).

The eschatological dimension of this pericope appears in verse 25 when Jesus says, "I shall not drink again the fruit of the vine until the day when I drink it new in the kingdom of God." The eucharist prefigures the Messianic banquet which will be shared by Jesus and his followers in the kingdom. This is a great promise of hope. The impending death of Jesus, which has been in the mind of the reader since the first death plot (3:6), will not be the final word. Jesus will have to suffer the pain of death, but his story will end with victory, not defeat, as he drinks the cup again in the kingdom of God.

Peter's Denial (14:27-31)

27 Then Jesus said to them, "All of you will have your faith shaken, for it is written: 'I will strike the shepherd, and the sheep will be dispersed.' 28 But after I have been raised up, I shall go before you to Galilee." 29 Peter said to him, "Even though all should have their faith shaken, mine will not be." 30 Then Jesus said to him, "Amen, I say to you, this very night before the cock crows twice you will deny me three times." 31 But he vehemently replied, "Even though I should have to die with you, I will not deny you." And they all spoke similarly.

The above scene completes the discipleship failure "sandwich" that surrounds the last supper. Just as Jesus had predicted the betrayal of Judas, so now he foretells the denial of Peter and the flight of all the disciples. As we saw in the central section of the Gospel, it is the suffering and death of Jesus that causes his disciples so much trouble. What is going to befall Jesus does not fit into their messianic hopes. When they realize that following Jesus does indeed mean the way of the cross they will flee from him.

Jesus adds that after he has been raised up, he shall go before them to Galilee (14:28). This refers either to an anticipated resurrection appearance (cf. 16:7) or to the parousia (cf. 13:24-27). In any case, Mark presents Jesus looking forward to a post-resurrection meeting with his disciples. Jesus prophesies not only the darkness of his death but also his resurrection and his eventual reconciliation with his disciples. Peter, as we have seen before, does not want to hear about death and resurrection (8:32). The passage ends with Peter vehemently protesting Jesus' claim that he would deny Jesus. He refuses to even contemplate the possibility of his failure. The other disciples likewise claim that they will not deny Jesus.

For reflection: Once again, the modern reader is challenged. Jesus does not fulfill ordinary human expectations of a Savior. Are you able to accept a suffering, dying, rising Messiah?

Jesus in Sorrow (14:32-42)

32 Then they came to a place named Gethsemane, and he said to his disciples, "Sit here while I pray." 33 He took with him Peter, James, and John, and began to be troubled and distressed. 34 Then he said to them, "My soul is sorrowful even to death. Remain here and keep watch." 35 He advanced a little and fell to the ground and prayed that if it were possible the hour might pass by him; 36 he said, "Abba, Father, all things are possible to you. Take this cup away from me, but not what I will but what you will." 37 When he returned he found them asleep. He said to Peter, "Simon, are you asleep? Could you not keep watch for one hour? 38 Watch and pray that you may not undergo the test. The spirit is willing but the flesh is weak." 39 Withdrawing again, he prayed, saying the same thing. 40 Then he returned once more and found them asleep, for they could not keep their eyes open and did not know what to answer him. 41 He returned a third time and said to them, "Are you still sleeping and taking your rest? It is enough. The hour has

come. Behold, the Son of Man is to be handed over to sinners. [42]Get up, let us go. See, my betrayer is at hand."

Eventually they arrive at Gethsemane and the disciples have their final chance to understand Jesus before his death. Peter, James and John are again singled out as they were at the Transfiguration (9:2-8) and the raising of the dead girl (5:37-43). They have seen Jesus in his glory, and now they see him in his weakness. Three times Jesus prays, and three times these disciples relax and sleep. Jesus' exhortation in the apocalyptic discourse (13:32-37) to "watch" takes on added significance here. Jesus is asking his disciples to keep awake spiritually as well as physically.

This is a very moving and powerful scene in Mark's Gospel. Jesus, who foretold his passion and death earlier in the Gospel (8:31-33; 9:30-32; 10:32-34) and has just declared that he is looking forward to a time after his death when he would drink wine anew in the kingdom of God (14:25), falls to the ground and prays that he will be delivered from that death (14:35). Troubled and distressed, Jesus' words to his disciples, "My soul is sorrowful even to death" (14:34), echo Psalm 42 (especially verses 6 and 12), which express a longing for God in the midst of suffering and fear of death.

Jesus' prayer that God would take away "this cup" clearly refers to his suffering and death (cf. 10:38-39; 14:23-24). Mark presents Jesus as the Son of God, as we saw earlier, yet he also portrays Jesus as a human being, who is fearful in the face of his impending death. This is not a contradiction. One can have foreknowledge about an impending crisis and accept God's will in the situation, yet still be fearful. Those suffering with terminal diseases (e.g., cancer) often evidence this mixture of faith and human weakness. In their anxiety, they pray for deliverance from death while at the same moment they are praying that God's will be done.

Mark portrays Jesus as completely submissive to the will of his heavenly Father. His closest followers are unable to stay awake and to comfort him during this difficult time. Mark presents Jesus as a model of prayer and obedience. The failure of the disciples in this pericope is indicated by Jesus' referring to Peter as Simon (14:37). Jesus has referred to this disciple as Peter ever since 3:16, when the reader learned that henceforth Simon would be called Peter. He, and by implication the others, is not the new Peter; he remains the old Simon.

For reflection: This passage causes us to reflect on the likelihood that we would betray Jesus if we found ourselves in a difficult situation. Peter, who boldly stated that even if he had to die he would not deny Jesus (10:31), is sleeping. So are James and John, who confidently asserted that they could drink the cup that Jesus drinks (10:38-39). This should serve us as a caution against arrogance and overconfidence. Jesus withstood the temptation to abandon the course set for him by God. We must recognize that we too will be tempted to stray from the path God would like us to walk. Perhaps Mark is suggesting that humility and prayer are needed by those who face temptation. Do you mistakenly think that you can withstand any temptation on your own?

Jesus Arrested (14:43-52)

⁴³ Then, while he was still speaking, Judas, one of the Twelve, arrived, accompanied by a crowd with swords and clubs who had come from the chief priests, the scribes, and the elders. ⁴⁴ His betrayer had arranged a signal with them, saying, "The man I shall kiss is the one; arrest him and lead him away securely." ⁴⁵ He came and immediately went over to him and said, "Rabbi." And he kissed him. ⁴⁶ At this they laid hands on him and arrested him. ⁴⁷ One of the bystanders drew his sword, struck the high priest's servant, and cut off his ear. ⁴⁸ Jesus said to them in reply, "Have you come out as against a robber, with swords and clubs, to seize me? ⁴⁹ Day after day I was with you teaching in the temple area, yet you did not arrest me; but that the scriptures may be fulfilled." ⁵⁰ And they all left him and fled. ⁵¹ Now a young man followed him wearing nothing but a linen cloth about his body. They seized him, ⁵² but he left the cloth behind and ran off naked.

While Jesus is speaking with his three intimate companions, Judas arrives with a crowd armed with swords and clubs. The armed mob has been sent by the chief priests, scribes and elders to arrest Jesus. The horror of Judas' treachery is highlighted by Mark's mention of the fact that Judas was "one of the twelve" (14:43) and Judas' use of a sign of friendship, a kiss (14:44), as the signal for betrayal. Shortly after he reports the arrest of Jesus, Mark informs the reader that "all left him and fled" (14:50). The male disciples disappear at this point in the story and, except for Peter's denial, do not reappear in this Gospel. If they achieve prominence later in the tradition it is because of God's grace and not due to any human characteristics of bravery or loyalty. Jesus has now been abandoned by his family, the religious authorities, and his closest male friends. The only group that does not desert him is the women, who watch the crucifixion and appear at the tomb expecting to anoint Jesus' body (15:40ff.).

Jesus Before the Sanhedrin (14:53-65)

53 They led Jesus away to the high priest, and all the chief priests and the elders and the scribes came together. 54 Peter followed him at a distance into the high priest's courtyard and was seated with the guards, warming himself at the fire. 55 The chief priests and the entire Sanhedrin kept trying to obtain testimony against Jesus in order to put him to death, but they found none. 56 Many gave false witness against him, but their testimony did not agree. 57 Some took the stand and testified falsely against him, alleging, 58 "We heard him say, 'I will destroy this temple made with hands and within three days I will build another not made with hands.'" 59 Even so their testimony did not agree. 60 The high priest rose before the assembly and questioned Jesus, saying, "Have you no answer? What are these men testifying against you?" 61 But he was silent and answered nothing. Again the high priest asked him and said to him, "Are you the Messiah, the son of the Blessed One?" 62 Then Jesus answered, "I am; and 'you will see the Son of Man seated at the right hand of the Power and coming with the clouds of heaven.'" 63 At that the high priest tore his garments and said, "What further need have we of witnesses? 64 You have heard the blasphemy. What do you think?" They all condemned him as deserving to die. 65 Some began to spit on him. They blindfolded him and struck him and said to him, "Prophesy!" And the guards greeted him with blows.

The Sanhedrin was the highest court and legislative body in Judaism. It was composed of priests, scribes (lawyers and theologians), and elders (the lay nobility). The two charges against Jesus are that he threatened to destroy the Jerusalem temple and that he committed blasphemy. Mark tells the reader that many lied and that there was considerable disagreement. Many witnesses speak against Jesus. Throughout the trial Jesus remains almost completely silent. It is likely that Mark is again presenting Jesus as the Suffering Servant, who stood silent before his captors (cf. Is 53:7).

The high priest asks Jesus if he is "the Messiah, the son of the Blessed One" and Jesus responds by speaking about the Son of Man, who will come with the clouds of heaven and be "seated at the right hand of the Power" (14:62). This is the second time that Jesus has been offered the title Messiah. Both here and in response to Peter's confession (8:29ff.), when he is offered this title he speaks instead about the Son of Man. As in the central section of the Gospel, someone addresses the titles Christ and Son of God to Jesus. While not rejecting those titles, Jesus emphasizes that to correctly understand him one must also see him as the Son of Man. Jesus' first response to the high priest's question is the "I am" we saw in 6:50 with overtones of the divine "I am" in Exodus 3:14. Mark thus keeps christology as his primary focus. "Messiah" remains a correct but inadequate title. "Son of God" and "I am" are superior but must be complemented by the title "Son of Man."

There are some serious historical problems with Mark's presentation of a full-scale trial having taken place in the high priest's house before the entire Sanhedrin on the first evening of Passover. The reader, however, must remember that Mark is interested in making a theological point, not an accurate reconstruction of the Jewish trial of Jesus. We have here neither a court stenographer's report nor a newspaper account of the trial of Jesus. What we find in Mark's Gospel is a theological statement about the ultimate meaning of Jesus' condemnation and death, whose present form has been influenced by passages from the Hebrew Scriptures (cf. Is 53:7; Ps 38:12-13) and later theological reflection on Jesus' crucifixion and resurrection. Those interested in historical reconstruction usually suggest that behind this trial scene is a strategy session, a preliminary hearing before a small group of Jewish leaders, that took place the evening before the first evening of Passover.

Peter's Denial (14:66-72)

66 While Peter was below in the courtyard, one of the high priest's maids came along. 67 Seeing Peter warming himself, she looked intently at him and said, "You too were with the Nazarene, Jesus." 68 But he denied it saying, "I neither know him nor understand what you are talking about." So he went out into the outer court. (Then the cock crowed.) 69 The maid saw him and began again to say to the bystanders, "This man is one of them." 70 Once again he denied it. A little later the bystanders said to Peter once more, "Surely you are one of them; for you too are a Galilean." 71 He began to curse and to swear, "I do not know this man about whom you are talking." 72 And immediately a cock crowed a second time. Then Peter remembered the word that Jesus had said to him, "Before the cock crows twice you will deny me three times." He broke down and wept.

In this final pericope of chapter 14, Mark returns to the story of Peter, last mentioned in 14:54. The contrast between Jesus, who openly proclaims the truth about himself, and Peter, who denies the truth about his relationship with Jesus, is obvious. Jesus confesses and dies; Peter denies and lives. As stated earlier, this serves as a warning to all Christians about human weakness and the potential to sin.

This is a very carefully crafted scene that rises in intensity from Peter's feigned ignorance to simple denial to a final denial and cursing. Three times Peter is accused of being one of Jesus' disciples, twice by the maid and once by the bystanders. Peter first claims not to know what the girl is talking about. After the second accusation, Peter is reported to have denied that he was one of Jesus' followers. This escalates into Peter's third response when he strengthens his denial with an oath. Peter begins to curse and swear that he does not even know Jesus. The disciple who had vowed never to deny Jesus (14:29-31) breaks down and weeps when he realizes the enormity of his failure.

Jesus Before Pilate (15:1-15)

15:1 As soon as morning came, the chief priests with the elders and the scribes, that is, the whole Sanhedrin, held a council. They bound Jesus, led him away, and handed him over to Pilate. 2 Pilate questioned him, "Are you the king of the Jews?" He said to him in reply, "You say so." 3 The chief priests accused him of many things. 4 Again Pilate questioned him, "Have you no answer? See how many things they accuse you of." 5 Jesus gave him no further answer, so that Pilate was amazed. 6 Now on the

occasion of the feast he used to release to them one prisoner whom they requested. [7] A man called Barabbas was
then in prison along with the rebels who had committed
murder in a rebellion. [8] The crowd came forward and
began to ask him to do for them as he was accustomed.
[9] Pilate answered, "Do you want me to release to you the
king of the Jews?" [10] For he knew that it was out of envy
that the chief priests had handed him over. [11] But the
chief priests stirred up the crowd to have him release
Barabbas for them instead. [12] Pilate again said to them in
reply, "Then what (do you want) me to do with (the
man you call) the king of the Jews?" [13] They shouted
again, "Crucify him." [14] Pilate said to them, "Why?
What evil has he done?" They only shouted the louder,
"Crucify him." [15] So Pilate, wishing to satisfy the crowd,
released Barabbas to them and, after he had Jesus
scourged, handed him over to be crucified.

The Sanhedrin handed Jesus over to Pilate, the Roman
prefect of Judea from 26 to 36 C.E., for questioning. While
the Jewish authorities have condemned Jesus to death, it is
implied that they did not have the authority to carry out
the sentence (cf. 14:64). It appears that in Mark's view the
primary blame for Jesus' death rests with the Jewish Sanhedrin. Pilate is portrayed as reluctant to condemn Jesus.
Most scholars today, however, would place the historical
blame more on the Roman authorities. The charge that led
to the crucifixion was that Jesus was the "king of the Jews."
This would have had serious political overtones in
first-century Roman Palestine. Pilate was legally responsible for Jesus' death by crucifixion. It was the Romans who
executed Jesus. Crucifixion was a Roman punishment
reserved for those thought to be rebels, slaves or bandits.
The careful reader of this Gospel will realize that the
Jewish leaders have acted exactly as Jesus had predicted in

his third passion-resurrection prediction: "The Son of Man will be handed over to the chief priests and the scribes, and they will condemn him to death and hand him over to the Gentiles, who will mock him, spit upon him, scourge him, and put him to death, but after three days he will rise" (10:33-34).

In the questioning of Jesus that takes place before Pilate, as in the trial before the Sanhedrin, Jesus reminds readers of the Suffering Servant (cf. Is 53:7), as he remains virtually silent. While Mark does not explicitly quote from the Suffering Servant songs in Isaiah, it is clear that his presentation of Jesus resembles that figure, who bore abuse in silence and atoned for the sins of the people. Pilate's question, "Are you the king of the Jews?" indicates that he is interested more in the political implications of the titles used for Jesus (e.g., Messiah and Son of God). To claim political kingship was treason, a capital offense. If it could be established that Jesus was connected with a messianic political movement, then Pilate could condemn him to death as a revolutionary. Jesus' enigmatic answer, "You say so" (15:2), allows Jesus to accept the ultimate truth of the title while denying its worldly political connotations. From Mark's perspective Jesus is the king of the Jews, the true Messiah, and much more. Jesus says nothing more to Pilate with regard to the charges brought against him.

Mark does not mention the fact that there must have been a trial before Pilate in which Jesus was declared guilty. Instead he presents Pilate as offering the crowd a choice between two condemned prisoners. The Barabbas incident again gives evidence that Mark wants to place the blame for Jesus' death on the Jewish leadership. There is no extrabiblical evidence of the custom referred to here of releasing a prisoner on the occasion of the Passover. Perhaps behind this scene is the occasional granting of a request for amnesty. Mark's point here is more important than this historical detail. Mark tells the reader that Barabbas was a rebel, who had committed murder. This means that the Jewish people are facing a critical decision. Will they choose the innocent Jesus and his understanding of messiahship or the insurrectionist with his political agenda? Urged on by their leaders (15:11ff.), the crowd demands that Jesus be crucified. In a sense this reminds us of a choice we all face. Those confronted by Jesus and his message must ultimately choose either to accept him or to reject him.

Pilate asks the crowd what evil Jesus has done (15:14). Although they can cite nothing, they call for Jesus' crucifixion. Pilate, "wishing to satisfy the crowd," has Jesus scourged (i.e., lashed with a leather whip containing pieces of bone or metal while bound to a pillar) and delivered to be crucified.

For reflection: Does Christian faith require a commitment to action on behalf of the poor and oppressed in an attempt to liberate them from the unjust social, economic, and political order in which they find themselves? If your answer is yes, then this pericope, with its account of the freeing of a revolutionary who has committed murder, offers you the opportunity to ask if rebellion and murder are acceptable means to use in order to achieve a more just society.

The Soldiers (15:16-20)

> [16] The soldiers led him away inside the palace, that is, the praetorium, and assembled the whole cohort. [17] They clothed him in purple and, weaving a crown of thorns, placed it on him. [18] They began to salute him with, "Hail, King of the Jews!" [19] and kept striking his head with a reed and spitting upon him. They knelt before him in homage. [20] And when they had mocked him, they stripped him of the purple cloak, dressed him in his own clothes, and led him out to crucify him.

Although Mark continues to be interested in the suffering of Jesus, the emphasis in this pericope is not on the pain and agony caused by the soldiers' actions. Mark draws the reader's attention to the actions of the soldiers that ironically proclaim the truth of Jesus' identity. They clothe Jesus in purple, the color worn by kings, and place upon his head a crown of thorns in order to mock Jesus' royal claim. They salute him as "King of the Jews" (15:18) and kneel down before him in mock homage (15:19). All six references in this Gospel to Jesus as the "king of the Jews (Israel)" occur in Mark 15 (15:2, 9, 12, 18, 26, 32). Although Mark has applied texts from Israel's royal Messianic tradition (e.g., Ps 2:7) to Jesus throughout the Gospel, he has this title applied explicitly to Jesus only in the climactic section of this story, when Jesus' true identity is revealed.

Mark believes that Jesus really is the king of the Jews. What is being emphasized here is a totally different understanding of kingship. Jesus is a king in a manner radically distinct from those "rulers over the Gentiles" who "make their authority felt" by lording it over others (10:42). The soldiers mock Jesus, because they see him as a weak and helpless pretender to the only kind of royal authority they have known. Jesus does not share their understanding of power and authority. His power is that of the Son of Man, who "did not come to be served but to serve and to give his life as a ransom for many" (10:45).

The Crucifixion and Death of Jesus (15:21-41)

> [21] They pressed into service a passer-by, Simon, a Cyrenian, who was coming in from the country, the father of Alexander and Rufus, to carry his cross. [22] They brought him to the place of Golgotha (which is translated Place of the Skull). [23] They gave him wine drugged with myrrh, but he did not take it. [24] Then they crucified him and divided his garments by casting lots for them to see what each should take. [25] It was nine o'clock in the morning when they crucified him. [26] The inscription of the charge against him read, "The King of the Jews."

As they led Jesus out to be crucified, Pilate's soldiers pressed into service Simon, a Cyrenian, to carry his cross. No reason is given why this was necessary. The condemned criminal normally carried the crossbar or transverse bar to the place of crucifixion. The upright pole would have remained fixed in place at Golgotha. After they arrive at the site of the crucifixion, they offer Jesus wine drugged with myrrh (a narcotic to kill the pain; cf. Prv 31:6-7). Mark does not indicate why Jesus refused to take the wine and myrrh.

Mark appears to have constructed chapter 15 according to a time sequence of three-hour intervals. The chapter begins with reference to daybreak (6 a.m.). Verse 25 reports that it was the third hour (9 a.m.), verse 33 that it was the sixth hour (noon) and midafternoon (3 p.m.), and verse 42 that it was evening (6 p.m.). This sequence, which may have been for liturgical or catechetical purposes, disagrees with chronologies mentioned in the other gospels, most notably with John 19:14, where Jesus is condemned at about noon. This serves to remind us, once again, that the gospel writers are concerned with the meaning of events and not with each and every detail.

The brutal event of the crucifixion itself is reported in the briefest of ways. Mark is not interested in the details but in the significance of Jesus' death. The clothes of the crucified person became the property of the executioners, so it is not surprising to read that the soldiers cast lots for Jesus' garments (15:24). In light of the important place Psalm 22 plays in Mark's passion narrative, this action by the soldiers undoubtedly should be seen as a fulfillment of Psalm 22:19.

We have pointed out several times that Mark constructs his narrative in such a way as to lead the reader to conclude that much of what happens is a fulfillment of prophecy. As we stated earlier, however, Mark does seem to view the characters in his story as freely acting moral agents; they are not puppets.

For reflection: Do you think that God used freely chosen human acts to accomplish God's purpose, even if the human actors had no intention to do so? Do you believe that God continues to act this way?

> [27] With him they crucified two revolutionaries, one on his right and one on his left. [28][29] Those passing by reviled him, shaking their heads and saying, "Aha! You who would destroy the temple and rebuild it in three days, [30] save yourself by coming down from the cross."

³¹ Likewise the chief priests, with the scribes, mocked him among themselves and said, "He saved others; he cannot save himself. ³² Let the Messiah, the King of Israel, come down now from the cross that we may see and believe." Those who were crucified with him also kept abusing him.

Once the soldiers had crucified Jesus between two revolutionaries, a first group of taunters begins to file past the cross, mocking Jesus with the charges raised against him in 14:58 about threatening to destroy the temple and challenging him to save himself. Their actions are an echo of Psalm 22:8.

The derision hurled at Jesus by the chief priests, the scribes and the crowd mirrors the charge of 14:61, that Jesus is claiming to be the Messiah, and is reminiscent of the different understandings of messiahship suggested in the exchange between Jesus and Peter at Caesarea Philippi (8:27-33). The conclusion of the opposition is that if Jesus were the Messiah, the king of Israel, he should be able to use his power to his advantage and to save himself from pain. It is inconceivable that the Messiah would find himself hanging on a cross and not be able to do anything about it. Throughout Mark's Gospel, Jesus has spoken about the necessity of his suffering, death and resurrection, and the fact that he has come to serve others, not to be served. Neither Peter, nor Judas, nor those mocking Jesus at the crucifixion understand that messiahship involves obedience to and trust in God, even when that includes suffering and death.

³³ At noon darkness came over the whole land until three in the afternoon. ³⁴ And at three o'clock Jesus cried

out in a loud voice, "Eloi, Eloi, lama sabachthani?" which is translated, "My God, my God, why have you forsaken me?" [35] Some of the bystanders who heard it said, "Look, he is calling Elijah." [36] One of them ran, soaked a sponge with wine, put it on a reed, and gave it to him to drink, saying, "Wait, let us see if Elijah comes to take him down."

The passion drama now moves to its climax. Mark tells us that at high noon darkness came over the whole land until three in the afternoon (15:33). The reader is undoubtedly meant to think of the darkness threatened for the final days. Jesus had earlier spoken about this phenomenon when, in his apocalyptic discourse, he talked about the events that would precede the coming of the Son of Man in glory: "In those days after that tribulation the sun will be darkened, and the moon will not give its light, and the stars will be falling from the sky, and the powers in the heavens will be shaken" (13:24-25). The darkness is a prophetic apocalyptic motif, which turns upside down the traditional theme of the Day of Yahweh. That day will not bring salvation but destruction, not light but darkness (cf. Am 8:9).

At 3 p.m. Jesus cried out in a loud voice using the first words, in Aramaic, of Psalm 22, "Eloi, Eloi, lama sabachthani?" Jesus expresses his feeling of having been abandoned by God, although he does not give up hope in God. Some who focus only on the words in Mark 15:34, "My God, my God, why have you forsaken me?" suggest that this is a cry of utter despair and that Jesus dies feeling totally abandoned by God. Mark's audience would not have made this mistake. The words are clearly from Psalm 22, which is typical of the psalms of lament found in the

Hebrew Bible. These psalms begin on a note of desperation and end on a note of joy and praise. It is not the cry of an atheist but of a believer. The suppliant believes that God has acted in the past on behalf of individuals and the nation and expresses confidence that God can act decisively in the present to alleviate the suffering. Lament does not stand by itself but moves from petition made out of distress to joyful praise of God.

Our own christology is brought into question in this scene because of the challenges that the Church has had to face over the years. The Council of Nicea (325 C.E.) defined the divinity of Jesus; the Council of Chalcedon (451 C.E.) defined his full humanity (in everything except sin). The problem over the centuries has been that opposition to the belief in the divinity of Jesus has been more widespread in scholarly circles. Therefore, in public statements about the incarnation the Church has had to insist on the divinity of Jesus. Unfortunately this has given some the impression that divinity is the only important issue. The result is that many Christians today do not sufficiently appreciate the humanity of Jesus. The temptation of some readers, therefore, could be to downplay the suffering of Jesus in this scene since, after all, he is the Son of God. Carried too far, this christology becomes Monophysitism or Docetism: Jesus is not really human but only appears to have taken on our human condition. Mark understands Jesus' suffering to be real; his pain and anguish are not a pretense. Jesus' use of Psalm 22, the cry of the Just One, should be seen as heartfelt and sincere.

For reflection: What is your christology? Do you believe that Jesus truly was or that he only appeared to be human?

If Jesus was not truly human, how can he function as a model or standard for your behavior? Do you believe that Jesus was divine or that he merely fulfilled a unique role in the history of the human race, calling attention to the demands of God's kingdom among us?

> [37] Jesus gave a loud cry and breathed his last. [38] The veil of the sanctuary was torn in two from top to bottom. [39] When the centurion who stood facing him saw how he breathed his last he said, "Truly this man was the Son of God!" [40] There were also women looking on from a distance. Among them were Mary Magdalene, Mary the mother of the younger James and of Joses, and Salome. [41] These women had followed him when he was in Galilee and ministered to him. There were also many other women who had come up with him to Jerusalem.

The moment of death comes quickly; Mark does not dwell on its details. Jesus is said to have uttered a loud cry, although the content of Jesus' outcry is not revealed. The veil mentioned in 15:38, is presumably the one hung before the holy of holies, setting the boundary for the inner sanctuary, the most sacred area of the temple (cf. Ex 26:33). It is in the holy of holies that the ark of the covenant was kept. No one was allowed to enter this sacred inner sanctuary except the high priest, and he could only enter once a year on the feast of Yom Kippur. The symbolic message is usually understood to mean that the death of Jesus has put an end to the temple cult and thus to the old covenant. The Jerusalem temple has been replaced in God's plan by the Christian community, which is open to people of all nations (cf. 11:17).

The christological high point of the Gospel is reached

when the centurion looks upon the dead body of the crucified Jesus and acknowledges him as the Son of God. He is
the first human being in the Gospel to do so. According to
Mark, the place to perceive Jesus' Sonship is not first of all
in glory but in his suffering and death. The words of the
centurion, "Truly this man was the Son of God" (15:39),
recall the opening words of the Gospel and one of Mark's
main themes. Jesus is not addressed by this title because of
his impressive teaching or his wondrous miracles, but
because he is hanging on the cross. Throughout the
Gospel, Mark has suggested that it is not possible to
understand who Jesus is if one does not accept his suffering and death. Mark's portrayal of the disciples' blindness
throughout the Gospel, therefore, should be seen as part
of his christological claim. It is not possible to understand
Jesus until we accept that his messiahship involved his suffering and death.

By placing this confession by a Gentile immediately
after the story of the rending of the temple veil, Mark has
suggested that with Jesus' death salvation is now available
to the Gentiles. Gentiles can become disciples and members of the kingdom of God. We saw this as an important
theme in our comments on Mark 4:35–8:21 (chapter 3,
above), especially in Jesus' taking pity on the "Gentile"
crowd after they had been with him "for three days" in the
second feeding story (8:2). The death and resurrection of
Jesus signals the beginning of the worldwide mission.
Access to God is now through Jesus, the Son of God, and
not through the Jerusalem temple cult.

The Women Disciples

As the story continues, Mark informs the reader that there were women looking on, who had followed Jesus in Galilee and who had come up with him to Jerusalem. These faithful witnesses, to the crucifixion and the laying of Jesus in the tomb, stand in contrast to the jeering crowds and the male disciples, who abandoned Jesus in Gethsemane (14:50). The fascinating thing is that the women are the most loyal disciples. Women, who could not function as witnesses in Jewish courts, are chosen as witnesses to the triumphant news of the resurrection (16:9). Mary Magdalene is a very important witness, because she saw Jesus die (15:40), watched when he was buried (15:47), and went to the tomb on Easter (16:1). Peter denies his association with Jesus as the rooster crows. The other male disciples flee when the going gets tough. The women, however, hang on to the bitter end. In Mark's so-called Longer Ending, it is Mary Magdalene to whom the risen Lord appears first (16:9).

For reflection: This pericope invites us to think about our own attitudes toward women, their role in society and in the Church. A glance at world history reveals that, for the most part, economic, social, political, and religious institutions have been male-dominated. Those males who have been in control of the linguistic and symbolic systems throughout history have continually viewed the contribution of most women to human existence as of secondary value. The good news is that a new understanding of women and women's place in social and ecclesial life has been developing for more than a century. What is the message of this pericope for us, in our unique time and place in history? How significant is it for you that the women are the only followers of Jesus who do not desert him?

Jesus' Burial (15:42-47)

[42] When it was already evening, since it was the day of preparation, the day before the sabbath, [43] Joseph of Arimathea, a distinguished member of the council, who was himself awaiting the kingdom of God, came and courageously went to Pilate and asked for the body of Jesus. [44] Pilate was amazed that he was already dead. He summoned the centurion and asked him if Jesus had already died. [45] And when he learned of it from the centurion, he gave the body to Joseph. [46] Having bought a linen cloth, he took him down, wrapped him in the linen cloth and laid him in a tomb that had been hewn out of the rock. Then he rolled a stone against the entrance to the tomb. [47] Mary Magdalene and Mary the mother of Joses watched where he was laid.

It was Jewish custom to bury the dead before sunset (cf. Dt 21:22-23) and not uncommon for a wealthy pious Jew like Joseph of Arimathea to take upon himself the responsibility to bury an apparently unattended body. Mark's emphasis in these verses appears to be the fact of Jesus' death. Pilate's questioning of the centurion about Jesus having died, followed by Joseph's wrapping of Jesus and laying him in a tomb, let the reader know that Jesus has truly died. There is no question of Jesus being in a coma or having gone into shock as a result of the crucifixion. Thus the three passion predictions which spoke about the death of the Son of Man have been fulfilled.

The Resurrection (16:1-8)

16:1 When the sabbath was over, Mary Magdalene, Mary, the mother of James, and Salome bought spices so that they might go and anoint him. 2 Very early when the sun had risen, on the first day of the week, they came to the tomb. 3 They were saying to one another, "Who will roll back the stone for us from the entrance to the tomb?" 4 When they looked up, they saw that the stone had been rolled back; it was very large. 5 On entering the tomb they saw a young man sitting on the right side, clothed in a white robe, and they were utterly amazed. 6 He said to them, "Do not be amazed! You seek Jesus of Nazareth, the crucified. He has been raised; he is not here. Behold the place where they laid him. 7 But go and tell his disciples and Peter, 'He is going before you to Galilee; there you will see him, as he told you.'" 8 Then they went out and fled from the tomb, seized with trembling and bewilderment. They said nothing to anyone, for they were afraid.

Mark's Gospel does not conclude with the death of Jesus but rather with the triumphant announcement of his resurrection. In the form we have it, Mark's Gospel ends with the discovery of the empty tomb and the message of the young man to the women who came to anoint Jesus (16:1-8).

The empty tomb by itself is no proof of the resurrection; it merely tells us that the tomb was empty. Matthew's version of this story, for example, indicates that the Jews claimed that the disciples had stolen the body of Jesus (cf. Mt 28:11-15). The empty tomb was necessary, of course, if Jesus' disciples were to proclaim his resurrection. While Mark does not include a resurrection appearance of Jesus in his Gospel, the comment of the young man in the white robe concerning Jesus, "He has been raised" (16:6), makes it clear that Mark understands Jesus to have been resurrected. The additional declaration of the young man, "He is going before you to Galilee; there you will see him, as he told you" (16:7) functions in a similar manner. Mark is well aware that the resurrection is the key to a correct understanding of Jesus. All three passion predictions include prophecies of the resurrection of Jesus.

Most scholars agree that Mark deliberately intended to end his Gospel at 16:8 with the words "for they were afraid." Why would Mark have chosen to end his story in this manner, without any story of a resurrection appearance? The usual answer is that Mark assumed a knowledge of the resurrection appearances among his readers. Instead of focusing on the resurrection, Mark wanted to draw attention to the suffering and death of Jesus and to the expected parousia. We have spoken several times about the importance of accepting the suffering and death of Jesus in order to have a correct understanding of him. Let us here deal with the expected second coming.

The Second Coming

A close reading of the three passion-resurrection predictions (8:31; 9:31; 10:33) suggests to some scholars that Mark sees the resurrection as a prelude to the parousia. Mark's reference to seeing Jesus (16:7) can also be read as a reference to the parousia and not to a resurrection appearance. This reading would suggest that Mark is more interested in the parousia, which he expects to take place soon (cf. 13:30), than he is in focusing on the resurrection. If this is the case, then the modern reader shares more in common with Mark's original reader than some have thought. Like Mark's first-century audience, many today who are aware of the resurrection appearances still struggle to accept a suffering Messiah and to look forward with joyful hope to his return.

Instead of a relatively literal acceptance of the apocalyptic scheme found in the New Testament, contemporary scholars often translate this eschatological imagery into more modern terms. Because we do not know when the end of the world is coming and we know little about how it will take place, we need not waste time uselessly speculating about it. It is important to note, however, that when most scholars speak about the end of the world they are not talking about its destruction, but rather its completion, its consummation and transformation. Many today, who look forward in hope to Christ's second coming, do not expect it to be an apocalyptic event in the future. The Church maintains that Christ's presence is already in the process of being realized in human history and is actively being brought about by human love and human striving to make the whole earth submissive to God's will. When the New Testament authors wrote about the parousia or return of Christ they were using the genre of apocalyptic to speak about the arrival of all things at their final destination according to God's plan. The second coming of Christ is, thus, the final definitive revelation of God's all-embracing love for the world.

This contemporary approach might remind us of Jesus' discourse in Mark 4. In that speech we learned that Jesus was the center of history, the bringer of God's kingdom. Although it is already in the world, the kingdom of God remains hidden at present. The growth parables and the fact that God is in charge of the timetable led to the conclusion that overwhelming success was inevitable at some time in the future. One could participate now in this hidden kingdom by accepting its reality and leading one's life according to Jesus' teachings. This growth and development model would identify the parousia with the coming of the kingdom of God in its fullness.

For reflection: Most Christians claim to believe in the second coming of Christ. But are they talking about a sudden apocalyptic inbreaking of God's kingdom or a gradual growth and development toward the final destination of all things according to God's plan? Could we speak about both an evolutionary model and a sudden, unexpected conclusion? What do you understand the term "parousia" to mean today? Does anticipation of these final events involve more than passive waiting on the part of Christians? Must the Christian be actively involved in the movement of history toward the coming of God's kingdom in its fullness?

Appendix
Later Endings
(16:9-20)

The Gospel of Mark as we have it in the Christian canon does contain some resurrection appearances. However, there is almost universal agreement among scholars that these verses were not part of the original Gospel. Both the internal and external evidence support this conclusion. The vocabulary and style in these verses are different from the rest of the Gospel; they are absent from the earliest and best manuscripts now available to us; and, they were absent from manuscripts in the patristic period. These verses were most likely composed in the second century based on traditions found, among other places, in Luke 24 and John 20. We should keep in mind, however, that these verses are part of canonical scripture, having been accepted in and by the universal Church.

How the scholar treats these verses depends on the critical stance adopted. The historical-critical approach that has served as the basis for our examination of Mark's Gospel is known as redaction criticism. This method recognizes the creative role that Mark exercised in shaping the material he inherited and in the overall composition of his work. As mentioned in the introduction, Mark is a true author with his own vocabulary, style and themes. The Gospel narrative we possess is the result of Mark's use of his sources, his own theological convictions, concerns, and interests and those of his intended audience.

Mark did not write these verses and did not intend them to be part of his Gospel. The redaction critic, therefore, would see them as irrelevant to any discussion of Mark's narrative. Since these verses do not appear to have existed until at least fifty years after Mark finished his Gospel, they can neither be used to talk about the Markan vocabulary and style nor about Markan intent and themes. This is why redaction critical studies of Mark's Gospel rarely even mention these verses, except in an appendix or epilogue.

We should recognize, however, that there are many different methods of biblical interpretation. The canonical approach, for example, which originated in the United States some twenty-five years ago, proceeds from the perception that the Bible should be viewed as a whole in order to arrive at conclusions that are truly theological. What really matters in this method is the final canonical form of the text or book. This conclusion, that only the final canonical form of a book is sacred scripture, serves to remind us that Mark 16:9-20 is considered sacred scripture by the Church. As such, Christians believe that these verses were committed to writing under the inspiration of the Holy Spirit and contain revelation. In a spiritual commentary on the canonical Gospel of Mark, it is therefore necessary and appropriate to analyze these verses. The approach taken will still be scholarly and not a subjective interpretation stemming from the imagination or intellectual speculation. However, keep in mind that these verses were not part of the original Gospel of Mark.

THE LONGER ENDING [9] When he had risen, early on the first day of the week, he appeared first to Mary Magdalene, out of whom he had driven seven demons. [10] She went and told his companions who were mourning and weeping. [11] When they heard that he was alive and had been seen by her, they did not believe. [12] After this he appeared in another form to two of them walking along on their way to the country. [13] They returned and told the others; but they did not believe them either. [14] (But) later, as the eleven were at table, he appeared to them and rebuked them for their unbelief and hardness of heart because they had not believed those who saw him after he had been raised. [15] He said to them, "Go into the whole world and proclaim the gospel to every creature. [16] Whoever believes and is baptized will be saved; whoever does not believe will be condemned. [17] These signs will accompany those who believe: in my name they will drive out demons, they will speak new languages. [18] They will pick up serpents (with their hands), and if they drink any deadly thing, it will not harm them. They will lay hands on the sick, and they will recover." [19] So then the Lord Jesus, after he spoke to them, was taken up into heaven and took his seat at the right hand of God. [20] But they went forth and preached everywhere, while the Lord worked with them and confirmed the word through accompanying signs.

THE SHORTER ENDING [And they reported all the instructions briefly to Peter's companions. Afterwards Jesus himself, through them, sent forth from east to west the sacred and imperishable proclamation of eternal salvation. Amen.]

The above passage consists of four parts: an appearance to Mary Magdalene, to two disciples on their way to the country, and to the eleven disciples at table, followed by a story of the ascension of Jesus. The appearance of the risen Jesus to Mary Magdalene is reminiscent of stories found in Matthew 28:9-10, Luke 24:10-11, and John 20:14-18. It is striking that Mary Magdalene is mentioned in five of the six resurrection narratives in the gospel tradition. She is, therefore, a major witness. The appearance narrated in Mark 16:9-11 can be seen as a reward for her fidelity. She stood by the cross of Jesus (15:40-41), saw where he was buried (15:47), and came to the tomb to anoint him (16:1). The faithfulness of Mary Magdalene stands in stark contrast to the actions of the male disciples, who fled after Jesus' arrest (14:50). These verses also highlight the fact of the resurrection. Mary Magdalene, who had known Jesus prior to his death, has seen him alive again.

The second appearance of Jesus is to two disciples as they walk along on their way to the country. This scene is reminiscent of the Emmaus story in Luke's Gospel (Lk 24:13-35). The intent of the author in saying that Jesus appeared "in another form" probably was to stress that the risen Jesus had undergone a change from the Jesus of the historical ministry. The twin themes of continuity (it is the same Jesus) and difference (a transformation has taken place) are found in all the resurrection narratives in the gospels and in Paul's comments about the resurrection body in 1 Corinthians 15:42ff. After this experience of the risen Jesus, these disciples return to the others and inform them of what has happened. As in the case of Mary Magdalene, however, they are not believed.

The third scene tells of an appearance of the risen Jesus to the eleven as they sat at table on Easter Sunday night. Jesus begins by reproaching them for their unbelief and hardness of heart and finally commissions them to preach the gospel throughout the whole world. This is reminiscent of Matthew 28:16-20, Luke 24:36-43, and John 20:19-23, 26-29. Jesus' rebuke is especially harsh here leading some to suggest that the writer of these verses attached paramount importance to belief in the resurrection.

The first words of Jesus in Mark's Gospel call for repentance and faith, "believe in the gospel" (Mk 1:15). It was mentioned earlier that what one understands to be the content of the "gospel" or "good news" depends on where one stands in time. For the original readers or hearers of Mark's Gospel and those coming after them, this "good news" includes the early Christian preaching about Jesus, the risen Christ. Belief in the resurrection of Jesus has been a crucial part of the Christian tradition from the earliest days. It is an essential stage in the incarnational mystery, which speaks of God entering into human life so that human beings may enter into divine life.

In the modern world, objections to the possibility of a resurrection are based primarily in philosophy and science and not in biblical exegesis, the interpretation of sacred texts. Although we can trace the idea of the resurrection back to the earliest days of the Church, we cannot prove that this Christian understanding of events corresponds to what really happened. This is a matter of faith.

It surprises some readers to learn that doubt is part of the resurrection appearances in all four gospels. In spite of the fact that the disciples see Jesus, they cannot believe that it is really him (Mt 28:17; Lk 24:37; Jn 20:14). This doubt or hesitation on the part of the disciples is answered by many proofs (cf. Acts 1:3). Sometimes it is the words of Jesus that reassure his followers (cf. Mt 28:18-20), while at other times it is Jesus' reference to seeing his hands and feet (cf. Lk 24:39) or side (cf. Jn 20:20, 24-29) or his eating a piece of baked fish (cf. Lk 24:42-43). In Mark 16:9ff., doubt is addressed by multiple appearances. Perhaps these writers are giving us a typical example of what following Jesus will mean until the coming of the kingdom in its fullness: believers are caught between belief and doubt.

For reflection: Do you believe in the resurrection of Jesus? Is your understanding overly subjective, ignoring the biblical accounts of the appearances and denying all bodily reality to the resurrection? Is it overly objective, understanding the resurrection to have been something akin to the resuscitation of a corpse? How comfortable are you with the bodily transformation model suggested in Mark 16:12 and elsewhere in the New Testament? How important is your belief in the resurrection for your understanding of Jesus and the kingdom of God?

Jesus, the risen Lord, sends the eleven to proclaim the gospel to all nations with baptism as the Christian initiation rite (16:15-16). A missionary charge, in which the risen Jesus entrusts a salvific mission to those to whom he appeared, is part of the resurrection appearances in each of the gospels (Mt 28:19-20; Lk 24:47; Jn 20:21). All people are to be invited to believe in Jesus.

One of the most emphatic statements in the New Testament about the relationship between baptism and salvation appears in verse 16, "Whoever believes and is baptized will be saved; whoever does not believe will be condemned." Baptism, then, is how one passes from the state of unbeliever to the state of being a disciple of Jesus. Mark tells us that Jesus himself was baptized by John (Mk 1:9-11), and because of that the Christian community became convinced that he approved of "a baptism for the forgiveness of sins" (1:4). Questions arise later in the tradition about the universal necessity of baptism based, in part, on Mark 16:16. Christians commonly believe that baptism is necessary for salvation; however, they often disagree on how this requirement can be fulfilled. Speculation concerning whether the unbaptized can be saved usually involves a discussion about water baptism, baptism by blood, baptism by desire, infant baptism, etc. Some Christians hold that since the offer of grace and revelation is universally available, baptism is necessary only for those explicitly called by God to become members of the Church. Perhaps it is best to say that Christian baptism is a participation in Jesus' baptism and an initiation into his mission. This text can be used to reflect on your own position on the universal necessity of baptism with its various implications.

The idea that Jesus' disciples will be given the power to perform marvelous works is found in many New Testament writings (e.g., Mt 21:21; Jn 14:12; Acts 3:6; 9:34, 40). These texts are usually talking about visible signs of God's presence, power, and love. Because they are similar to events in the life of Jesus, they suggest that the mission of Jesus is continued in the ministry of the Church. The physical healing of the afflicted is sometimes seen as a foretaste of the resurrection from the dead and a sign that salvation encompasses the whole person.

Many people living at the turn of this century have considerable difficulty understanding miracles. The basic problem is that we have a very different world view than those living in the first-century Mediterranean world. Jesus' contemporaries personified nature and saw God as having absolute control over it. God was responsible for everything that happened and, therefore, anything was possible. God's intervention in human history, always awe-inspiring, was viewed as a sign of God's mercy and power. As surprising as God's intervention was, it was very much in keeping with God's nature. The modern scientific world has separated nature from God and claims that nature operates by its own independent laws. God is far removed from the scene, and if God enters human history at all via the miraculous, these events are seen as contrary to the laws of nature.

For reflection: What is your attitude toward modern scientific scepticism about the possibility of miracles? Are you comfortable talking about God's loving and caring presence in nature and history? Are you aware of any visible signs of God's presence, power, and love? What signs are there today that the Church is continuing the mission of the Spirit-filled Jesus?

The final section of this appendix to Mark's Gospel deals with the ascension of Jesus and is reminiscent of Luke 24:50-51 and Acts 1:9-11. On Easter Sunday evening (Mk 16:9), as he was seated at table with his disciples (16:14), Jesus was taken up into heaven (cf. 2 Kgs 2:11) and took his seat at the right hand of God (cf. Ps 110:1). Jesus will no longer be physically present with his disciples. Now enthroned in glory, the risen Lord is with his disciples in a different manner. He works with them and confirms the word of their missionary preaching through accompanying signs (16:20). The reader is left looking forward in hope to the successful missionary campaign of the Church and to the parousia.

For reflection: Do you live with a similar hopeful anticipation that the gospel will be spread successfully throughout the entire world and that finally God's will for creation will be realized?

For Further Reading

Achtemeier, Paul J. *Invitation to Mark*. Garden City, NY: Image Books, 1978.

_____. *Mark*. Proclamation Commentaries. 2d edition. Philadelphia: Fortress Press, 1986.

Barta, Karen A. *The Gospel of Mark*. Message of Biblical Spirituality 9. Wilmington, DE: Michael Glazier, 1988.

Donahue, John R. *The Theology and Setting of Discipleship in the Gospel of Mark*. Milwaukee: Marquette University, 1983.

Flanagan, Patrick J. *The Gospel of Mark Made Easy*. Mahwah, NJ: Paulist Press, 1997.

Hare, Douglas R. A. *Mark*. Westminster Bible Companion. Louisville, KY: Westminster John Knox Press. 1996.

Harrington, Wilfrid. *Mark*. New Testament Message. Wilmington, DE: Michael Glazier, 1979.

Hooker, Morna D. *The Gospel According to St. Mark*. Black's New Testament Commentaries. London/Peabody, MA: A & C Black/Hendrickson, 1991.

Humphrey, Hugh M. *He is Risen! A New Reading of Mark's Gospel*. Mahwah, NJ: Paulist Press, 1992.

Hurtado, Larry W. *Mark*. A Good News Commentary. San Francisco: Harper & Row, 1983.

Juel, D. H. *Mark*. Augsburg Commentary on the New Testament. Minneapolis, MN: Augsburg, 1990.

Kelber, Werner. *Mark's Story of Jesus*. Philadelphia: Fortress Press, 1979.

Kilgallen, John J. *A Brief Commentary on the Gospel of Mark*. New York/Mahwah, NJ: Paulist Press, 1989.

Matera, Frank. *What Are They Saying about Mark?* New York: Paulist Press, 1987.

McBride, D. *The Gospel of Mark. A Reflection Commentary*. Dublin: Dominican Publications, 1996.

Rhoads, David, and Donald Michie, *Mark as Story*. Philadelphia: Fortress Press, 1982.

Telford, W. R. *Mark*. New Testament Guides. Sheffield, UK: Sheffield Academic Press, 1982.

Williamson, Lamar. *Mark*. Richmond: John Knox Press, 1983.